Turn today into the start of your love transformation!

Unlock deeper connections and attract the romance you deserve.

100 Feng Shui Love Tips to Improve your Love life.

Michele

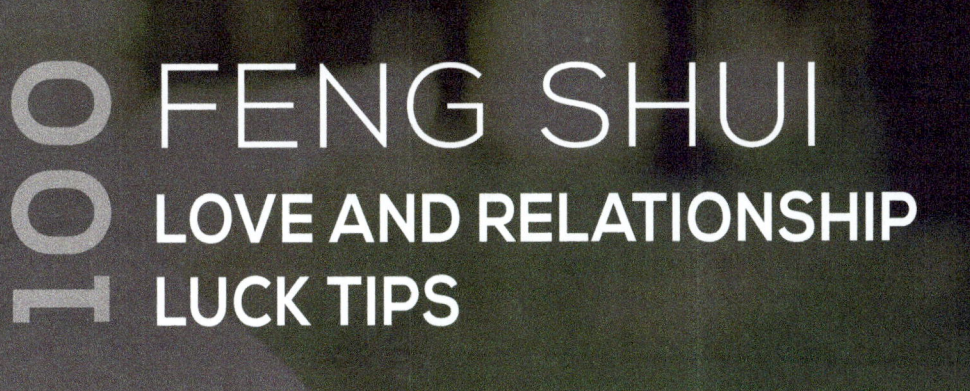

100 FENG SHUI
LOVE AND RELATIONSHIP LUCK TIPS

100 FENG SHUI LOVE AND RELATIONSHIP LUCK TIPS

Published by Complete Feng Shui
Mb: 0421 116 799,
Email: info@completefengshui.com.au
Websites: www.fengshuilove.shop; www.completefengshui.com

100 Feng Shui Love and Relationship Luck Tips©
TEXT COPYRIGHT © MICHELE CASTLE
ILLUSTRATIONS COPYRIGHT © MICHELE CASTLE

All rights reserved. No part of this publication may be reproduced, stored in a retrieval system or transmitted in any form or by any means, electronic, mechanical, photocopying, recording, or otherwise, without the prior written permission from Complete Feng Shui.

The author's moral right to be identified as the author of this book has been asserted.
Author: Michele Castle
Design copyright © completefengshui
Title: 100 Feng Shui Love and Relationship Luck Tips

ISBN: 978-0-6459097-5-3 (Paperback)
ISBN: 978-0-6459097-6-0 (Hardcover)
ISBN: 978-0-6459097-7-7 (EPUB)
October 2024

This book provides valuable insights and guidance for aligning with your home energies of Form, Flying Stars, Bagua, and Chinese astrology. The author, editor, and publisher disclaim any responsibility for outcomes resulting from applying the information in this book.

The information in this book is summarised using the Flying Star, Bagua, Form and Four Pillars of Destiny Formulation as per the Chinese Thousand Year Calendar. It is presented in a user-friendly way to help you enjoy prosperity throughout the year.

Vice President of the Association of Feng Shui Consultants (AFSC) Platinum member of the Association of Feng Shui Consultants (AFSC) Recognised Feng Shui training institution by the (AFSC)

 facebook@completefengshui   instagram@completefengshui

Book Cover, Book Layout & eBook Conversion by manuscript2ebook.com

SUCCESS STORIES:
TRANSFORMING LOVE AND RELATIONSHIPS WITH FENG SHUI

Readers who have applied the principles in the 100 Feng Shui Love and Relationship Luck Tips guide and experience positive changes in their love lives and relationships.

"This guide completely transformed my love life!"
I had been struggling to find the right partner, but after using some tips in this book, like clearing the clutter in my Southwest corner and placing rose quartz in my bedroom, I started attracting more meaningful connections. Within months, I met someone who aligns with my values and goals! – *Samantha B.*

"Our relationship has never been stronger."
My partner and I were going through a rough patch, so I decided to try the feng shui tips for our bedroom. After adjusting the bed position and adding more romantic touches, we felt an immediate improvement in our communication. Now, we're closer than ever! – *James & Eliza H.*

"I was sceptical at first, but the results were amazing."
I never thought something as simple as changing my home's layout could impact my love life, but the results were undeniable. After following the tip to add soft lighting and balance the energy in my bedroom, my relationship with my partner became more harmonious and loving. – *Natalie P.*

"Perfect for single people looking to manifest love."
As someone who has been single for a while, this book helped me shift my mindset and my home's energy to be more inviting to love. The tip about creating a love vision board and activating my love corner was a game changer—I've been attracting positive romantic opportunities ever since! - *Tom R.*

"The changes were immediate and profound."
My husband and I decided to try some of the feng shui tips to bring more balance into our relationship. After clearing out old items and introducing a pair of Mandarin ducks, the atmosphere in our home lightened up, and we've been communicating better ever since! - *Michelle L.*

"Finally found the missing piece for relationship harmony."
I've read a lot about feng shui, but this guide was the first one that truly helped me apply it to my love life. After enhancing the Southwest corner of my apartment, I felt an incredible shift in my energy, and within weeks, I reconnected with an old flame. We're now in a committed relationship! - *Alex M.*

"A practical, easy-to-follow guide for improving love energy."
This book made it so easy to integrate feng shui into my home, and the results were fast! I added red accents in my bedroom and followed the steps to remove emotional blockages—and now my partner and I feel more passionate and connected than ever. - *Tina W.*

"I'm amazed at how feng shui shifted my relationship."
I implemented the suggestion to clear the clutter under our bed and balance the space with matching bedside lamps, which made a noticeable difference in our relationship dynamics. The emotional tension between us eased, and we've been much more aligned ever since. - *Rebecca G.*

"A must-have for anyone looking to improve their love life."
I followed the advice to introduce the Double Happiness symbol and balanced my relationship area with earth tones. Not only did my home feel cozier, but I also started to attract healthier relationships into my life. This guide is a true blessing! - *Jason L.*

"Brought new energy into my marriage.
" My wife and I have been married for over 15 years, but things have become stagnant. After following the tips in this book to enhance our bedroom's energy, we've reignited our spark and feel more connected than ever before. - *David T.*

"Such a fun and transformative guide!"
"I didn't realise how much my home affected my love life until I read this book. After removing mirrors from my bedroom and introducing gentle lighting, our relationship took on a new level of connection and intimacy. I highly recommend it!" – *Sophie D.*

"Helped me find peace after a breakup."
After a difficult breakup, I used the tips in this book to clear negative energy from my home. Placing heart-shaped crystals and introducing soft, nurturing elements helped me heal and attract new love. I'm grateful for the changes it brought! – *Megan F.*

CONTENTS

About the Author: Michele Castle	10
Introduction	13
Understanding Feng Shui	17
The Bagua Map—Your Blueprint for Enhancing Love and Relationship Luck	22
Self-Realisation for Love and Relationship Growth	28
Tips 1 - 100	34
Feng Shui Love and Relationship Luck Checklist	85

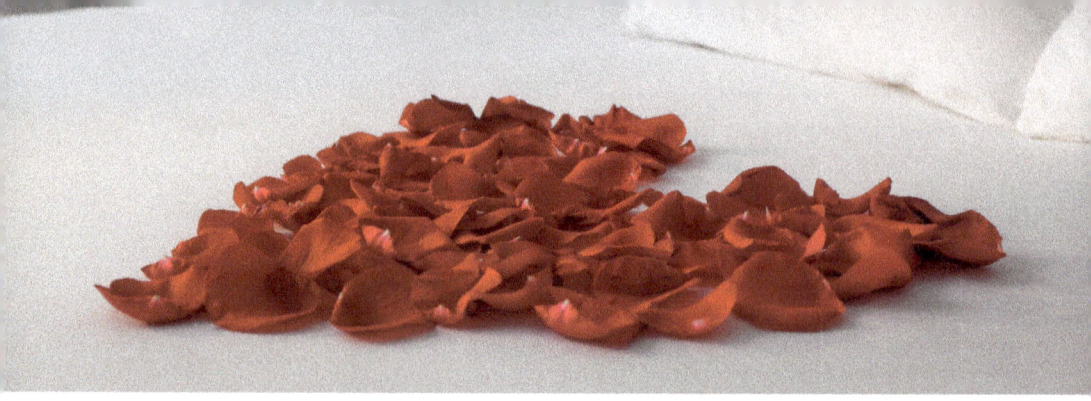

ABOUT THE AUTHOR: MICHELE CASTLE

Michele Castle is a renowned Feng Shui expert, life coach, and transformational speaker with decades of experience helping individuals align their environments with the powerful energy of love, abundance, and personal fulfilment. With a deep passion for Eastern metaphysical sciences, Michele has dedicated her career to sharing the ancient wisdom of Feng Shui, Chinese astrology, and holistic living practices with modern audiences. Her work is rooted in the belief that our homes are mirrors of our inner worlds, and by making intentional changes in our environment, we can transform every aspect of our lives—especially our relationships. When applied correctly, Feng Shui can create a harmonious and balanced environment that supports personal growth and fulfilment.

Michele's journey into Feng Shui is a testament to the transformative power of this ancient art. Her quest for answers to life's challenges led her to traditional home organisation and design methods. However, the discovery of Feng Shui truly opened her eyes to the profound connection between space and well-being. Inspired by the positive changes in her life, such as a significant improvement in her relationships and a boost in her career, Michele delved deep into the study of Feng Shui, eventually becoming one of Australia's most sought-after consultants and teachers in the field. Her unique practical knowledge and spiritual insight blend have helped thousands unlock their full potential by creating harmonious, love-filled environments. Michele's journey reflects the transformative power of Feng Shui, making her teachings relatable and inspiring.

As the author of several Feng Shui books, including works on Chinese astrology and the energy dynamics of the home, Michele brings a wealth of knowledge and personal experience to her readers. She is also a retreat facilitator, the founder of

Complete Feng Shui, and a leader in holistic festivals, such as the Festival of Love and the Festival of Healing, where she brings together wellness practitioners, healers, and spiritual seekers to explore the transformative power of energy work.

The **Feng Shui 100 Love and Relationship Tips** testify to Michele's commitment to sharing practical yet spiritually grounded tools for personal transformation. These tips, an extension of her work as an author and teacher, offer simple, accessible Feng Shui principles to enhance love and relationships. Michele created this treasure of a book to empower individuals to use their surroundings' energy to cultivate more fulfilling and harmonious romantic lives.

Michele's work goes beyond simply decorating a space—transforming the home's energy to manifest one's deepest desires, especially in love. Drawing from her extensive knowledge of Feng Shui and her journey in life and love, Michele designed this book as both a practical guide and a tool. This book can be used practically as a quick reference and guide to assess and enhance your home's energy and spiritually connect with the more profound energies of love and passion. She believes that when our homes are in harmony, love can flow freely, and through this book, she hopes to inspire others to create environments that support joy, connection, and passion.

When Michele is not teaching workshops, writing books, or consulting on Feng Shui projects, she is actively living the principles she shares. She firmly believes in the power of intention, self-love, and creating spaces that nurture growth, healing, and connection. Michele's vision is to help individuals worldwide discover the magic of Feng Shui and use it to live their best, love-filled lives. Her belief in the transformative power of intention and self-love is a source of inspiration for those who seek to create positive changes in their lives.

Michele's love for the art of Feng Shui and her passion for helping others shine through in everything she does. Her unwavering commitment to her work is a testament to her dedication, and she is honoured to share this transformative guide with you. Through this guide, she invites you to take your love journey to the next level and experience the power of aligning your home with the energy of love and romance. Michele's dedication to her work ensures that you are in good hands as you embark on your journey of personal transformation.

Feng Shui can help bring about changes in many areas of your life.

- Career
- Fame
- Prosperity
- Relationships
- Family
- Helpful people
- Mentors
- Travel
- Personal growth
- Creativity
- Knowledge
- Education
- Health and well being

Start by writing a statement of intention and commitment.

....
....
....
....
....
....
....
....
....
....

INTRODUCTION

UNLEASHING THE TRANSFORMATIVE POWER OF THE 100 FENG SHUI LOVE AND RELATIONSHIP LUCK TIPS

Welcome to the **100 Feng Shui Love and Relationship Luck Tips**, a guide that holds the transformative power of feng shui. It's designed to help you turn your environment into a sanctuary of love, attraction, and relationship success. Drawing on the ancient principles of feng shui, these 100 tips provide a robust, practical roadmap to create balanced, harmonious spaces that nurture and enhance your romantic and emotional well-being.

Each tip offers actionable insights rooted in feng shui principles that are remarkably easy to implement in your home. Whether you're seeking to attract new love, strengthen an existing relationship, or heal from past emotional wounds, this guide will help you foster deeper connections and align your space with the energy of love, empowering you to take control of your romantic and emotional well-being.

What Is This Guide About?

The **100 Feng Shui Love and Relationship Luck Tips** are designed to bring you closer to the energies of love, harmony, and emotional connection. Inside, you will find a practical, hands-on approach that you can easily apply to your daily life, providing reassurance and confidence in the effectiveness of these tips.

1. **Reflective Questions**: These questions help you explore aspects of your love life and home energy, encouraging introspection on emotional blocks, relationship dynamics, and the energetic flow in your space.

2. **Feng Shui Insights**: Each tip offers detailed feng shui wisdom, guiding you to create environments that support love on physical, emotional, and spiritual levels.

3. **Practical Actions**: Each tip provides easy-to-follow steps to align your home's energy with your relationship goals—whether you want to attract new romance, strengthen your current partnership, or heal from past heartaches.

How to Use This Guide

This guide can be used in various ways, depending on your intentions and needs. Whether you are new to feng shui or an experienced practitioner, these tips offer valuable insights to help you create a space that enhances love and connection. Here are some ways to work with the guide:

1. Daily Guidance

Start your day by selecting a tip to improve the love energy in your home. Reflect on the question and implement the suggested action. This daily practice helps you stay mindful of your environment and how it influences your relationship energy.

2. Love or Relationship Enhancement

If you have a specific area of concern in your love life, turn to the tip that speaks to that issue. Each tip provides direct insight into enhancing that part of your relationship. The reflective questions will guide you in understanding your emotional needs, while the feng shui advice offers practical steps to address them.

3. Room-by-Room Feng Shui Adjustments

Use this guide to focus on particular rooms in your home that impact your relationship luck, such as the bedroom, living room, or the Southwest corner, which governs love and relationships. Follow the feng shui tips to bring more harmony and love-enhancing energy into these critical areas.

4. Relationship Manifestation

If you want to attract new love, use the tips as part of your manifestation process. Select the ones that resonate most with your goals and follow the actions to create a space that invites love and romance. You can also keep this guide handy as a reminder of your intention to welcome love into your life.

5. Strengthening Your Current Relationship

For couples looking to deepen their connection, this guide offers practical ways to create a home environment that supports emotional closeness and harmony. Work together on the suggested actions to realign your home's energy and foster mutual respect, understanding, and love.

Creating Your Love Space

Your home reflects your inner world. Small, intentional changes in your physical environment can dramatically shift your life's flow of love energy. Feng shui teaches love thrives in balanced, clutter-free, and harmonious spaces. This guide will help you transform your home into a nurturing haven for love.

From clearing clutter and energising critical areas like the Southwest Corner to incorporating love-enhancing elements such as crystals for clarity, flowers for beauty and life, and colours like red for passion and pink for romance, you'll learn how to create a space that supports your relationship goals.

Practical Tips for Maximising the Guide

- **Create a Ritual**: When using the guide, take a moment to centre yourself. Light a candle, burn incense, or sit quietly to focus your intentions. This practice will help you connect more deeply with the guidance. Flip open the guide and pick a page.

- **Journal Your Progress**: Track the insights and actions that resonate most with you. Journaling allows you to reflect on any shifts in your relationship dynamics or home energy as you apply feng shui principles. "Journal your progress in The Feng Shui Love Journal" available https://www.barnesandnoble.com/w/the-feng-shui-love-journal-michele-castle https://bit.ly/3BGfXXO

- **Act**: Each tip in this guide provides a specific action to improve your love energy. Implement these changes in your home, and watch how they bring positive results into your relationship.

- **Revisit Tips Regularly**: Feng shui is an ongoing practice. Check with the guide to ensure your home's energy aligns with your love goals. You may find that certain areas need readjusting as your relationship evolves.

CONCLUSION: ALIGNING WITH LOVE ENERGY

The **100 Feng Shui Love and Relationship Luck Tips** are a powerful tool for anyone looking to enhance their love life through feng shui. By applying these tips, you transform your environment and intend to attract more love, harmony, and joy.

May this guide support your journey to creating more profound, more fulfilling connections, and may your space be filled with the energy of love and happiness.

Enjoy the journey, and let the wisdom of feng shui lead you to more excellent romance, connection, and emotional well-being.

UNDERSTANDING FENG SHUI

Feng Shui, often called the "art of placement," is an ancient Chinese practice that seeks to harmonise individuals with their surrounding environment. Its philosophy is rooted in the understanding that the energy, or "chi," that flows through our homes and personal spaces is directly connected to the power that flows through our lives. By aligning our environment with Feng Shui principles, we can create balance, enhance well-being, and manifest our deepest desires—particularly love, relationships, and personal fulfilment. This transformative power of Feng Shui gives us hope and inspiration to improve our relationships.

In its simplest form, Feng Shui translates to "wind" (feng) and "water" (shui). These two elements are integral to life, constantly in motion, and can shape our world. Much like the wind and water, the energy around us continually moves, and Feng Shui teaches us how to harness this energy to promote harmony and success. The ultimate goal of Feng Shui is to balance the five natural elements—wood, fire, earth, metal, and water—within your living space so that the energy, or chi, flows freely and positively through your environment.

The Core Philosophy of Feng Shui

At its core, Feng Shui is based on the idea that everything is interconnected. Our surroundings, personal energy, and the universe's energy are in constant dialogue. When our external environment is balanced, it can positively influence our internal world, bringing clarity, peace, and, most importantly, alignment with our desires.

Feng Shui emphasises that energy exists in two primary forms: **yin** and **yang**. Yin represents the passive, feminine, and calming energies, while yang represents the active, masculine, and stimulating forces. Neither yin nor yang is superior to the other; instead, they must coexist harmoniously to create balance. In a relationship, this could manifest as balancing emotional support and independence or nurturing and passion to ensure that both partners contribute equally to and receive from the relationship. This balance reassures us about the natural dynamics of our relationships.

Another central aspect of Feng Shui is the **Bagua**, an energy map that divides the home into different sections, each corresponding to a specific area of life—such as wealth, career, health, and relationships. The Bagua is a powerful tool that allows us to pinpoint which areas of our home are related to our love life. Understanding the Bagua and making conscious adjustments to these areas, particularly the Southwest corner, can enhance the energy flow and create a more supportive environment for our relationships. This enlightenment about the Southwest corner can guide us in creating a more harmonious space for love.

Understanding Chi: The Flow of Life Energy

Chi, often described as "life force" or "universal energy," flows through everything—our homes, bodies, and world. When chi flows smoothly, it brings harmony, good health, and balance to all aspects of life. However, when chi is blocked, stagnant, or weak, it can manifest as stress, conflict, or dissatisfaction in relationships and other areas of life.

In Feng Shui, chi is influenced by how we arrange our environment, the colours we choose, the materials we surround ourselves with, and the placement of furniture and objects. The philosophy is that everything in your space either promotes or hinders the flow of chi, and by mindfully designing your surroundings, you can ensure that chi flows in a way that supports your emotional and physical well-being.

For example, if the flow of energy in your bedroom—the space most closely linked to love and relationships—is disrupted by clutter or harsh elements like sharp corners, it can create tension and conflict in your romantic life. Similarly, suppose the energy in your Southwest corner (the area of the home associated with love and marriage) is weak or stagnant. In that case, it can delay or disrupt the arrival of new love or strain an existing partnership.

The Five Elements in Feng Shui: Their Role in Relationships

The five elements—wood, fire, earth, metal, and water—are the foundation of Feng Shui. Each element represents a different type of energy, and by balancing these elements in your environment, you can harmonise the power in your relationships. Let's explore each element and its influence on love:

1. **Wood**: Wood symbolises growth, vitality, and flexibility. In relationships, it represents emotional growth and adaptability. Bringing wood into your space through plants, wooden furniture, or green hues can help relationships flourish and promote healthy communication.

2. **Fire**: Fire is the element of passion, warmth, and transformation. It ignites excitement and emotional intensity in relationships. Using the fire element—such as candles, red and orange tones, or artwork with triangular shapes—can enhance intimacy, strengthen passion, and bring warmth into a relationship.

3. **Earth**: The earth element stands for stability, grounding, and nurturing. It brings emotional security and helps relationships feel rooted and long-lasting. You can incorporate earth energy through ceramics, earthy colours like beige and terracotta, and square-shaped objects, encouraging commitment and trust in relationships.

4. **Metal**: Metal is associated with clarity, precision, and focus. It enhances communication and helps partners maintain clear boundaries and mutual respect. Metal elements like round shapes, metallic decor, or white and grey colours can bring harmony and open, honest dialogue to a relationship.

5. **Water**: The water element embodies flow, emotions, and intuition. It promotes emotional depth and connection between partners. Bringing water elements into your space through fountains, mirrors, or shades of blue can help nurture empathy and emotional understanding.

Each element uniquely influences your space and relationships, and Feng Shui teaches us how to balance these elements to create a supportive environment for love. Too much of any one element can create an imbalance—for example, too much fire can cause conflict, or too much water can lead to emotional overwhelm. Harmonising all five elements is essential for a well-rounded, fulfilling love life, and understanding the potential adverse effects of an imbalance can help us avoid these pitfalls.

Feng Shui and the Importance of Clutter Clearing

Clutter clearing is one of the most basic yet powerful principles of Feng Shui. Clutter represents stagnant energy, and in the context of love and relationships, it can create emotional blockages, confusion, and a lack of clarity in your romantic life. Feng Shui teaches that a cluttered space leads to a cluttered mind, making it difficult to attract or maintain a healthy relationship.

Clutter in critical home areas, such as the bedroom or the Southwest corner, blocks the flow of positive love energy. It can symbolise unresolved emotional issues, attachment to past relationships, or a lack of space for new love to enter your life. By clearing clutter, you allow chi to flow freely, creating space for love, growth, and connection.

Clearing clutter isn't just about physical objects—it's also about clearing emotional and energetic clutter. This can mean letting go of old memories, photos, or items from past relationships that no longer serve you. When you clear out these remnants of the past, you create energetic room for new love to enter or for current relationships to evolve in healthier, more positive ways.

The Southwest Corner: Your Relationship Power Spot

In Feng Shui, the Southwest corner of your home represents love, relationships, and marriage. This area is one of the most essential spaces for cultivating relationship energy. By activating and nurturing the power in this part of your home, you can attract love into your life or enhance the emotional bond with your current partner.

Feng Shui suggests incorporating elements symbolising love and harmony to energise the Southwest corner. These can include pairs of objects (such as two candles, two hearts, or two figurines), symbols of love like mandarin ducks, and colours like pink and red. Ensuring this space is clean, clutter-free, and filled with positive love symbols will amplify your home's relationship energy flow.

If you feel that your love life is stagnant or lacking fulfilment, it's worth evaluating and enhancing the energy in your Southwest corner. When aligned with Feng Shui principles, the space can become a powerful magnet for love and emotional connection.

Applying Feng Shui to Love and Relationships

The beauty of Feng Shui is that it offers practical, tangible steps anyone can take to improve their environment and, by extension, their relationships. You don't need to make drastic changes all at once; instead, you can make minor, intentional adjustments that gradually align your space with the energy of love and harmony.

The **100 Feng Shui Love and Relationship Luck Tips** guide you through these adjustments, helping you identify areas in your home that may hinder the flow of love energy and offering solutions to restore balance. Whether you're seeking new love, trying to deepen an existing relationship, or simply looking to bring more harmony into your home, these cards offer a wealth of Feng Shui wisdom to support your journey.

Feng Shui is ultimately about connection to your environment, personal energy, and the universal flow of love and abundance. By understanding and applying the principles of Feng Shui, you can transform your home into a sanctuary of love, creating a space where relationships can thrive and where you can attract the love you desire.

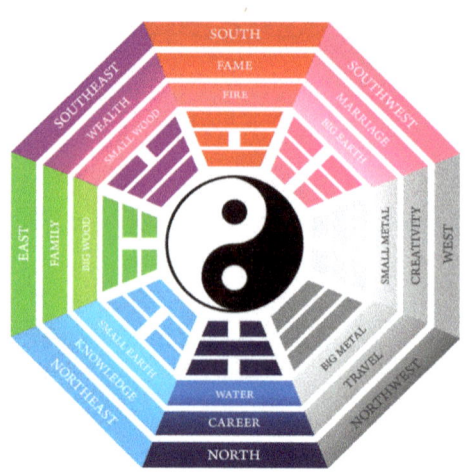

THE BAGUA MAP–

YOUR BLUEPRINT FOR ENHANCING LOVE AND RELATIONSHIP LUCK

The Bagua Map is at the core of feng shui, a potent tool that is an energetic blueprint for your home and life. The Bagua divides your living space into nine key areas, each representing a crucial aspect of your life: wealth, career, health, and love and relationships. By comprehending and working with the Bagua, you can consciously activate the areas of your home that influence your romantic life. Activation in this context means to enhance or stimulate the energy flow in a particular area, thereby inviting more profound love, harmonious partnerships, and emotional connection into your life.

This chapter will provide a detailed exploration of the Bagua, focusing on how to use it to enhance your love and relationship luck. We will delve into the specific area of the Bagua dedicated to relationships—the Southwest—and how this powerful zone, when activated, can attract or strengthen love. Understanding the significance of the Southwest corner will help you stay focused and determined in your love enhancement journey.

What is the Bagua?

The **Bagua** (pronounced "bah-gwah") is an ancient feng shui tool used to map out the energetic blueprint of your home or space. Each of the nine sections of the Bagua corresponds to a specific life area:

1. **Wealth & Prosperity** (Southeast)
2. **Fame & Reputation** (South)

3. **Love & Relationships** (Southwest)
4. **Family & Health** (East)
5. **Children & Creativity** (West)
6. **Knowledge & Self-Cultivation** (Northeast)
7. **Career & Life Path** (North)
8. **Helpful People & Travel** (Northwest)
9. **Center/Health** (Center)

When overlaid on the floor plan of your home, the Bagua reveals which areas correspond to different aspects of life. Enhancing energy in a specific section of the Bagua can positively influence that part of your life. For love and relationship luck, the Southwest corner is of utmost importance. Still, as we'll see, the other sections of the Bagua also play a crucial role in creating a balanced and loving environment. This understanding will reassure you and keep you optimistic about the potential for love enhancement in your home, instilling a sense of hope and positivity.

How to Use the Bagua Map in Your Home

When you begin working with the Bagua, the first step is to align the Bagua map with your home's layout (refer to Bagua map at the back of this book). Traditionally, the Bagua is aligned with the main entrance of your home. This means that when you stand at your front door looking into your home, the **Career & Life Path** area will align with the front centre of your home, while the **Love & Relationships** area will align with the back left corner of your home.

Once you've aligned the Bagua to your home's layout, you can identify the specific areas corresponding to different aspects of your life. To enhance love and relationships, the critical area to focus on is the Southwest corner, but don't overlook how other sectors can influence your love life. For instance, the **Centre** governs overall harmony and health, which are crucial for a loving relationship, while the Southeast influences wealth, which can also impact the stability of a relationship. Understanding these connections will reassure you and keep you optimistic about the potential for love enhancement in your home.

The Southwest: The Love and Relationship Corner

The **Southwest** sector of your home, a vital area of the Bagua, is dedicated to **love, romance, partnerships, and marriage**. This is where the energy of relationships is most potent, and it directly influences how love flows into your life. Whether you're looking to attract a new partner, strengthen an existing relationship, or bring more harmony into your home, activating the Southwest corner is essential.

In feng shui, the Southwest corner is associated with the **Earth element**, symbolising grounding, stability, and nurturing. It is the foundation for creating lasting, harmonious relationships. To enhance your love and relationship luck, it's essential to cultivate a supportive and positive energy in this area. Here are some key ways to activate the Southwest corner for love:

1. Declutter and Cleanse the Space

The first step to activating any area of the Bagua is to ensure it is free from clutter and negative energy. Clutter in the Southwest corner represents unresolved emotional baggage or obstacles in your love life. By clearing out unnecessary items, you create space for new love or allow existing relationships to flourish.

Smudging the area with sage, ringing a bell, or using essential oils can further cleanse the energy and prepare the space for love-enhancing activations.

2. Enhance with Earth Elements

Since the Earth element governs the Southwest, it's essential to incorporate symbols and materials that resonate with grounding, nurturing energy. This could include:

- **Earthy tones**: Use colours such as beige, terracotta, soft yellow, or brown to create a warm, stable environment.

- **Crystals**: Place grounding crystals like rose quartz (for love) or amethyst (for emotional clarity) in this corner to amplify loving energy.

- **Ceramic and stone objects**: Incorporate ceramic vases, stone sculptures, or clay figurines to strengthen the Earth element and stabilise your romantic relationships.

Refer to page 99 at back of book for Bagua cut out to overlay on your floor plan.

3. Introduce Pairs

In feng shui, pairs symbolise balance, harmony, and relationship equality. By placing paired objects in the Southwest corner, you can enhance the energy of partnership and union. Some examples include:

- **Two candles**: Lighting two candles in this corner can symbolise the light and warmth of a balanced relationship.

- **Two hearts or figurines**: Objects in pairs, such as two hearts, doves, or artwork depicting a couple, can invite unity and harmony into your love life.

- **Mandarin ducks** are traditional feng shui symbols of love and loyalty. A pair of mandarin ducks in the Southwest corner can help attract or strengthen a committed relationship.

4. Use Romantic Colors

In feng shui, colours such as pink, red, and peach are associated with love and passion. These tones can activate romantic energy in your Southwest corner. Whether you paint a wall, use pillows, or incorporate artwork in these shades, the key is to use them thoughtfully to evoke feelings of love and attraction.

5. Include Symbols of Love

Symbols of love can significantly enhance the energy of the Southwest corner. This could include:

- **Rose quartz**: Known as the stone of unconditional love, rose quartz is ideal for attracting new love or deepening existing emotional bonds.

- **Double happiness symbol**: This traditional Chinese symbol is often used to promote love and marital bliss. Placing this symbol in the Southwest corner can help enhance joy and happiness in your romantic life.

Other Key Bagua Areas for Love Enhancement

While the Southwest is the primary area for love and relationships, other areas of the Bagua also play essential supporting roles in cultivating a harmonious and balanced romantic life:

1. Centre: Health and Harmony

The Centre of your home represents overall health and harmony, and it's essential to keep this area clear and balanced to support all aspects of your life, including relationships. A cluttered or neglected Centre can create an imbalance in your love life. Ensure this area is clean and peaceful, as it acts as the heart of your home, influencing how you feel emotionally and physically in your relationships.

2. Southeast: Wealth and Prosperity

The Southeast area governs wealth and abundance; financial stress can often impact relationships. Activating this corner can bring prosperity, which may help alleviate financial pressures in a relationship and create a more stable environment for love to flourish.

Enhance this area with wood elements, such as plants, and symbols of wealth, such as coins or prosperity bowls. When your financial life is stable, your relationship can benefit from reduced stress and tension.

3. Northeast: Knowledge and Self-Cultivation

The Northeast corner represents personal growth, knowledge, and wisdom. Personal development is crucial for long-term success in a relationship. Activating this area encourages both partners to focus on self-improvement and introspection, helping to create a stronger, more balanced union.

Incorporate symbols of learning, such as books or crystals like lapis lazuli, to encourage personal growth that enriches your relationship.

4. Northwest: Helpful People and Travel

This area governs connections with others, including mentors, family, and friends. A supportive network can provide valuable advice and emotional support for a relationship, so activating this corner with symbols like a globe or travel souvenirs can help cultivate connections that benefit your love life.

Working with the Bagua for Lasting Love

The Bagua map is not just a static tool; it's a dynamic way to interact with the energy in your home and life. By regularly assessing and adjusting the power in the different areas of the Bagua, you can continuously enhance your love and relationship luck. As your life evolves, so too should your space. Regularly updating and refreshing the energy in key Bagua areas ensures that your environment remains a positive force in your romantic journey.

The Bagua becomes even more powerful when used alongside the 100 Feng Shui Love and Relationship Tips. Each tip offers specific actions to activate love energy in your space, and by applying these tips to the relevant areas of the Bagua, you can create a deeply aligned and harmonious environment that supports your heart's deepest desires.

Remember, feng shui is a holistic practice. When all areas of the Bagua are balanced, your relationships will reflect that harmony, creating space for love, joy, and fulfilment to grow.

SELF-REALISATION FOR LOVE AND RELATIONSHIP GROWTH

Before we can fully invite love into our lives or enhance the quality of our relationships, we must embark on a journey of self-reflection and personal growth. Love and relationships, at their core, are mirrors—reflecting not only our desires and dreams but also our fears, unresolved emotions, and areas of personal development. This chapter will guide you through a self-review process, using powerful questions that help unlock a deeper understanding of who you are in love, what patterns may be holding you back, and how you can align yourself more fully with the love you wish to attract or nurture.

These questions are not just questions; they are tools for transformation. They are designed to facilitate a journey of self-realisation, foster awareness, healing, and personal transformation, and create a foundation for better relationships. As you ponder each question, reflect deeply, journal your responses, and consider how the answers may reveal new insights about your love life and relationship dynamics. This journey is not just about understanding but about transformation, and it's a journey worth taking.

The Importance of Self-Realisation in Love

At the heart of every relationship lies your relationship with yourself. How you perceive yourself—your worth, boundaries, strengths, and vulnerabilities—shapes how you relate to others. Your self-awareness is not just a tool; it's a powerful force that influences the energy you bring into a relationship, your ability to communicate openly, and your capacity for self-love.

Feng shui teaches us that the energy of our home reflects our internal energy. Similarly, the love and relationships we experience reflect our internal emotional landscape. Self-realisation is not just a process; it's a path to aligning your inner world with the love you wish to create or attract. It's a journey worth taking, starting with turning inward and recognising your patterns. This journey is about understanding and actively shaping the love you want in your life.

Below are a series of questions designed to help you cultivate deeper self-awareness. Answering these questions honestly and openly will allow you to identify areas where you may need healing, growth, or clarity. By understanding yourself more profoundly, you will be better equipped to align with the energy of love and create a more fulfilling and harmonious relationship. This self-awareness is not just a tool; it's a powerful force you can harness to shape your relationship.

QUESTIONS FOR SELF-REALISATION IN LOVE

1. How do I define love, and what does it mean to me?

Love means different things to different people. For some, it may be about connection and emotional intimacy, while for others, it may be about security, companionship, or shared values. Understanding your definition of love helps you recognise whether the relationships you are in (or the ones you attract) align with your deepest needs and desires.

Reflection: Take time to explore what love truly means to you. Write down your definition of love and consider whether your current relationship or vision for love matches that definition.

2. What are my core beliefs about love and relationships?

Your beliefs about love shape the way you approach relationships. These beliefs can be empowering or limiting, depending on your past experiences and what you've internalised. Are you someone who believes love requires effort and sacrifice? Do you think love is easy, or do you have fears about vulnerability and trust?

Reflection: Consider your beliefs about love and relationships. Are these beliefs helping or hindering your ability to experience love fully? Identify limiting beliefs and consider how you can reframe them to create a more open, positive outlook on love. Reframing can open up new possibilities for growth and love in your relationships.

3. What patterns do I notice in my past relationships?

The patterns we experience in relationships often repeat themselves until we become conscious. These patterns might involve how you handle conflict, how open you are to receiving love, or how much you give versus how much you receive. Recognising patterns can clarify areas where you may need to break free of old habits.

Reflection: Look at your past relationships and identify recurring patterns. Are there themes that keep showing up, such as fear of commitment, communication challenges, or emotional detachment? What steps can you take to break these patterns and create healthier dynamics in your current or future relationships? Recognising and breaking free from these patterns empowers you to make more nutritious and fulfilling relationships.

4. How do I express love and affection?

Each person has a unique way of expressing love, whether through words of affirmation, acts of service, physical touch, or spending quality time together. Understanding your love language helps you communicate more effectively with your partner and ensures your needs for love and affection are met.

Reflection: Consider how you express love and how you prefer to receive it. Are you clear about your love language? How well does your partner (or potential partners) understand your need for affection, and how can you communicate this more openly?

5. What are my emotional triggers in relationships?

Emotional triggers are moments when we react strongly, often because they touch on deeper wounds or unresolved feelings from the past. If not addressed, these triggers can cause conflict or distance in relationships. Understanding your triggers is the first step to healing and preventing unnecessary emotional reactions.

Reflection: Identify moments when you feel emotionally triggered in relationships. What situations or behaviours tend to bring up strong reactions in you? How can you become more mindful of these triggers and respond in healthier, more balanced ways? For example, if criticism triggers feelings of inadequacy, you can practice self-compassion and remind yourself of your worth in these moments.

6. What are my boundaries in love, and do I communicate them?

Healthy boundaries are essential for maintaining balance and mutual respect in relationships. Without boundaries, you may give too much or allow behaviours that don't align with your values. Setting boundaries helps protect your emotional well-being and fosters respect from your partner.

Reflection: Reflect on the boundaries you set in relationships. Do you communicate them clearly to your partner or often compromise your boundaries to avoid conflict? What steps can you take to establish firmer boundaries, honouring your needs while respecting your partner? You can start by clearly articulating and discussing your boundaries with your partner, then consistently enforcing them respectfully and non-confrontationally.

7. Do I feel worthy of love and connection?

At the core of many relationship struggles is the issue of self-worth. If you do not feel deserving of love, you may sabotage relationships, settle for less than you deserve, or feel insecure about your partner's commitment. Recognising your worth is crucial for attracting and maintaining healthy, fulfilling relationships.

Reflection: Ask yourself whether you genuinely believe you are worthy of love, respect, and emotional connection. If not, where do these feelings of unworthiness come from, and how can you begin to heal and affirm your self-worth? Consider practices like self-compassion, positive affirmations, or therapy to support this journey.

8. How do I handle conflict and disagreement in relationships?

Conflict is a natural part of any relationship, but how you handle it can strengthen or weaken the bond. Some people avoid conflict at all costs, while others confront issues head-on. Reflecting on your approach to conflict can help you develop healthier ways to resolve disagreements and deepen mutual understanding.

Reflection: Think about how you typically handle conflict in your relationships. Are you open to communication and compromise, or do you avoid difficult conversations? How can you constructively approach conflict, allowing for growth rather than division?

9. Am I open to giving and receiving love equally?

Love is an energy exchange, and a healthy relationship requires both partners to give and receive love in balance. Sometimes, people over-give in relationships, while others struggle to receive love due to fear or past hurt. Ensuring that love flows both ways is essential for sustaining a fulfilling relationship.

Reflection: Consider whether you are open to giving and receiving love equally. Do you find yourself giving more than you receive, or vice versa? How can you restore balance in this area, ensuring you and your partner feel nourished by the relationship?

10. What are my greatest fears in love?

Fear is a powerful force in relationships, and it often manifests as a fear of rejection, abandonment, or vulnerability. These fears can lead to self-sabotage or prevent you from fully embracing love when it arrives. You can work through your fears and create a more open-hearted approach to love by identifying them.

Reflection: What fears arise when you think about love and relationships? Are these fears based on past experiences, or do they come from a more profound emotional place? How can you begin to face and release these fears to create more space for love to thrive?

Creating Space for Growth and Healing

By reflecting on these questions, you take the first step toward creating a more conscious and fulfilling relationship with yourself and others. Self-realisation is an ongoing process, and as you grow in awareness, you will begin to see how your internal shifts can positively influence your external relationships.

This chapter is designed to complement the wisdom of the **100 Feng Shui Love and Relationship Luck Tips,** helping you align your inner and outer worlds to create the love life you desire. The tips will guide you through transforming your physical environment. At the same time, self-reflection exercises will help you clear emotional blockages, develop healthier relationship habits, and open your heart to more profound, authentic love.

Remember, the journey to a better relationship starts with you. Embrace the process of self-realisation, and trust that as you grow, so will the love and connection in your life.

Tip 1: Activate the Southwest Corner

Question to Ponder: How can I bring more love and harmony into my relationship?

Answer: In feng shui, the southwest corner of your home governs love, relationships, and romance. By energising this area, you create an inviting space for love to flourish. This area represents Earth energy, grounding relationships and building strong emotional connections.

Action: Start by clearing clutter from the Southwest corner. Place objects in pairs (e.g., two candles, two hearts, two doves), symbolising partnership and unity. Use Earth and Fire elements like rose quartz, red candles, or ceramic figures. Make this space feel inviting, and regularly refresh the energy by cleaning and occasionally rotating the items.

Tip 2: Declutter the Bedroom for Love Luck

Question to Ponder: Is my bedroom a sanctuary for love or cluttered with distractions?

Answer: Clutter in your bedroom blocks the flow of love and intimacy. It disrupts the peaceful and romantic energy needed to nurture close relationships. Your bedroom should be a sanctuary where love can bloom without obstacles or distractions.

Action: Remove all unnecessary items from your bedroom, including work-related objects, electronics, or anything that does not serve a relaxing, intimate environment. Pay special attention to areas under the bed that can block energy flow. Replace clutter with items symbolising love and togetherness, like paired candles or soft textures.

Tip 3: Balance Yin and Yang Energy

Question to Ponder: How can I create harmony between independence and togetherness in my relationship?

Answer: Relationships thrive when there is a balance between yin (feminine) and yang (masculine) energies. Too much of one and not enough of the other can lead to disharmony. Both energies must coexist to foster a sense of wholeness and mutual respect in the relationship.

Action: Assess your home for the balance of these energies. Incorporate soft textures and flowing fabrics (yin), such as silk drapes or plush rugs, alongside more structured items (yang) like straight-edged furniture or angular decor. Achieving this balance in your home mirrors the balance needed for a relationship to thrive.

Tip 4: Rose Quartz for Romance

Question to Ponder: How can I nurture love in my life with the power of crystals?

Answer: Rose quartz is the stone of unconditional love and emotional healing. Its gentle pink colour aligns with the energy of the heart chakra and encourages feelings of love, compassion, and forgiveness. It helps attract new love or deepens an existing relationship.

Action: Place a rose quartz crystal in the Southwest corner of your home or bedroom. You can also wear it as jewellery to keep love energy with you throughout the day. Place a small piece under your pillow to encourage loving thoughts while you sleep to enhance its power.

Tip 5: Equal Space on Both Sides of the Bed

Question to Ponder: Is there equality and balance in my relationship space?

Answer: The bedroom reflects the balance between partners. If one side of the bed is blocked or has limited space, it may symbolise an imbalance in the relationship dynamic. Both partners need equal access and room to feel empowered.

Action: Ensure there is equal space on both sides of the bed. Remove any obstacles that block one side. Place matching bedside tables and lamps to symbolise equality in the relationship if possible. This minor adjustment can promote feelings of fairness and partnership.

Tip 6: Warm, Romantic Colors in the Bedroom

Question to Ponder: How can I use colour to create a more passionate and intimate environment?

Answer: The colours in your bedroom can significantly influence your relationship's energy. Warm, inviting colours like pink, red, and peach encourage feelings of love, passion, and connection. These colours stimulate romance and create an environment conducive to emotional bonding.

Action: If your bedroom feels cold or impersonal, consider introducing warmer colours. Start with bedding, pillows, or artwork in soft pink or peach tones. If you feel bold, paint an accent wall in a deep, rich red to ignite passion. Ensure these colours complement the overall energy of the room and reflect your relationship goals.

Tip 7: Avoid Mirrors Facing the Bed

Question to Ponder: How can I ensure my relationship is accessible from outside interference or disturbances?

Answer: In feng shui, mirrors are potent objects that reflect and double energy. When placed opposite the bed, they can invite third-party interference into your relationship, symbolically doubling people or drawing external distractions into the love space.

Action: If your mirror faces your bed, consider relocating it. If this isn't possible, cover the mirror at night with a cloth to prevent any disturbances to your relationship. This simple adjustment creates a more peaceful, intimate environment for you and your partner.

Tip 8: Display Symbols of Love

Question to Ponder: What visual reminders can I use to encourage love and connection?

Answer: Surrounding yourself with symbols of love helps keep the energy of romance alive. These symbols act as visual cues, constantly reminding you to focus on love, harmony, and connection. They can be handy for attracting new love or strengthening an existing relationship.

Action: Incorporate artwork and objects symbolising love, such as hearts, couples, or serene romantic landscapes. These can be placed in the Southwest corner or other prominent areas of your home where you spend time. Make sure these symbols evoke positive emotions and align with your love aspirations.

Tip 9: Enhance the Love Altar with Paired Objects

Question to Ponder: How can I create a sacred space to nurture love and emotional connection?

Answer: A love altar is a dedicated space to honour and nurture love energy in your life. By placing paired objects here, you create a powerful visual representation of partnership and togetherness, helping to attract or sustain love.

Action: Set up a small table or shelf in a quiet area of your home, preferably in the Southwest corner, and place paired objects such as two candles, two rose quartz crystals, or two hearts. Light the candles or meditate near the altar daily to strengthen the energy of love.

Tip 10: Keep the Southwest Corner well-lit

Question to Ponder: How can I use light to keep the energy of love alive?

Answer: Light is a crucial activator of positive energy in feng shui. A well-lit Southwest corner ensures the power of love and relationships is vibrant and active. Dim or dark spaces stagnate the flow of love energy, making it harder for romantic opportunities to manifest.

Action: Ensure your Southwest corner is well-lit with soft, warm lighting, such as lamps, candles, or fairy lights. Avoid harsh, cold lighting in this space. The key is to create a gentle, glowing atmosphere that invites love to flourish.

Tip 11: Remove Electronics from the Bedroom

Question to Ponder: Are the distractions in my bedroom preventing a deep connection with my partner?

Answer: Electronics like TVs, computers, and phones create distractions and emit energy that disrupts the peaceful, intimate environment needed for nurturing relationships. They can distract attention from meaningful conversations and quality time with your partner.

Action: Remove or minimise the presence of electronics in your bedroom. If a TV or computer is necessary, cover it with a cloth when not in use to reduce its energetic impact. Dedicate your bedroom solely to rest, intimacy, and connection. Create an electronics-free zone during certain hours to prioritise relationship time.

Tip 12: Use Peonies for Romance Luck

Question to Ponder: How can I symbolically invite romance and admiration into my life?

Answer: Peonies are powerful feng shui symbols of beauty, romance, and admiration. These flowers represent youthful love and blossoming relationships, especially helpful for singles seeking new love or couples looking to reignite passion.

Action: Display peonies in your home—fresh, artificial, or as artwork—especially in the Southwest corner or bedroom. Their lush, full blooms carry the energy of romance and invite suitors or increased affection from your partner. Replace or refresh the flowers regularly to keep love energy blooming.

Tip 13: The Importance of Headboard Stability

Question to Ponder: Does the foundation of my relationship feel secure and supported?

Answer: In feng shui, the headboard represents the support and stability in a relationship. A solid, sturdy headboard signifies a strong, supportive partnership, while a flimsy or missing one may indicate instability or lack of security.

Action: Ensure that your bed has a solid, high-quality headboard attached. It should be made from wood or upholstered fabric, symbolising unity and support. Avoid headboards made from metal rods or ones with gaps, as they represent division and weakness in relationships.

Tip 14: Avoid Sharp Corners in the Bedroom

Question to Ponder: Are the energies in my bedroom nurturing or harsh?

Answer: Sharp corners, particularly those pointing toward the bed, create "sha chi" or cutting energy, which can cause tension and conflict in relationships. These harsh angles disrupt the gentle, flowing energy that love needs to grow.

Action: Check your bedroom for furniture or decor with sharp corners pointing toward the bed. Soften the space by repositioning the items or covering the corners with fabric or plants. Opt for rounded, soft-edged furniture and accessories that promote smooth, harmonious energy.

Tip 15: Utilize the Power of Mandarin Ducks

Question to Ponder: How can I attract loyal, committed love?

Answer: Mandarin ducks are a classic feng shui symbol of love, devotion, and fidelity. They represent lifelong partnerships and are often used to attract or strengthen committed relationships. Keeping a pair in your home can invite stable, loyal love into your life.

Action: Place a pair of mandarin duck figurines in the Southwest corner of your bedroom or living space. Ensure they are displayed together, symbolising unity and commitment. If you're single, this can help attract a long-term partner. For couples, it reinforces the bond of love and loyalty.

Tip 16: Feng Shui for the Bed's Position

Question to Ponder: Is the positioning of my bed supportive of love and intimacy?

Answer: In feng shui, the position of your bed can significantly influence your relationship energy. A bed in the command position (where you can see the door but are not directly in line with it) ensures you feel secure, empowered, and open to receiving love.

Action: If your bed isn't in the command position, try to rearrange the room so you have a clear view of the door while lying in bed. Avoid placing the bed directly under a window or aligned with the door, as this can disrupt restful sleep and harmony in your relationship. If repositioning isn't possible, use a headboard and keep the door closed at night.

Tip 17: Remove Past Relationship Mementos

Question to Ponder: Am I still holding on to energy from past relationships?

Answer: Objects from past relationships, such as gifts, photos, or souvenirs, can carry old emotional energy that may block new love from entering your life. Holding on to these items can keep you energetically attached to the past, preventing you from moving forward in your love life.

Action: Inventory your home and bedroom for items connected to past relationships. Consider removing or donating these objects to create space for new love. If there are sentimental items you wish to keep, store them in a place far from your bedroom to reduce their energetic impact.

Tip 18: Introduce Fire Element for Passion

Question to Ponder: How can I reignite passion in my relationship or love life?

Answer: The Fire element represents passion, excitement, and intensity in feng shui. Introducing the Fire element into your home can help reignite the flames of love and bring more warmth into your romantic life.

Action: Add Fire element decor, such as candles, red or orange accents, or items with triangular shapes, into your bedroom or the Southwest corner of your home. Lighting candles during romantic moments or using warm lighting in your bedroom can strengthen the passion between you and your partner.

Tip 19: Clear Negative Energy Regularly

Question to Ponder: Am I holding on to negative emotional energy that could be blocking love?

Answer: Negative energy, whether from arguments, past hurts, or stress, can linger in your home and block the flow of love energy. Regularly clearing this stagnant energy is essential for maintaining an open, loving space.

Action: Use techniques such as smudging with sage or palo santo, ringing bells, or playing harmonious music to clear negative energy from your home, especially in the bedroom and Southwest corner. Do this regularly, particularly after conflicts or emotional upsets, to ensure your space remains open to love and positive connections.

Tip 20: Keep the Bed Accessible from Both Sides

Question to Ponder: Does my bedroom setup support equal partnership?

Answer: The bed represents the heart of a relationship. When one side of the bed is blocked or inaccessible, it can symbolise imbalance or control issues in the relationship. Both partners should have equal access to the bed, reflecting equality in love.

Action: Make sure both sides of the bed are easily accessible. Clear any obstacles that might block one partner's side, such as furniture, clutter, or walls. This adjustment fosters a sense of balance and equality in the relationship, promoting mutual respect and shared responsibility.

Tip 21: Avoid Water Elements in the Bedroom

Question to Ponder: Could the elements in my bedroom be drowning the passion in my relationship?

Answer: In feng shui, the Water element can symbolise emotional depth, but if overemphasised in the bedroom, it can weaken passion and intimacy. However, by making these changes, you can transform your space and potentially rekindle the love in your relationship. Too much Water energy in a space meant for rest and romance may lead to emotional coldness or relationship stagnation. Still, you can bring warmth and vitality back into your bedroom with the proper adjustments.

Action: You are responsible for maintaining the balance of elements in your bedroom. Remove large bodies of water, such as aquariums or water-themed artwork, and avoid having blue tones dominate the decor. Instead, focus on Earth or Fire elements to ground the relationship and bring warmth. Use Water elements sparingly in living areas where flow and calmness are desired.

Tip 22: Strengthen Earth Element for Stability

Question to Ponder: Does my relationship feel grounded and secure, or do I need more stability?

Answer: The Earth element in feng shui represents grounding, stability, and permanence. Adding Earth energy to your home or bedroom helps stabilise relationships, fostering long-term security and trust between partners.

Action: Incorporate Earth elements into your decor, such as ceramics, pottery, or stone objects. Earth tones like beige, brown, or terracotta are ideal for creating a sense of stability and warmth. Place these items in the Southwest corner or areas where you want to enhance the feeling of grounded love.

Tip 23: Check for Poison Arrows

Question to Ponder: Are there hidden sources of tension and conflict in my home?

Answer: In feng shui, "poison arrows" are sharp angles or objects pointing toward essential areas like your bed. They create negative energy that can lead to conflict or tension in relationships. These sharp lines direct harsh energy toward you, impacting the flow of love and harmony.

Action: Walk around your home and check for sharp corners from furniture, walls, or objects pointing toward your bed or other essential relationship areas. Soften these edges with plants and fabrics or by repositioning the furniture. This will help neutralise negative energy and restore peace and balance in your relationship.

Tip 24: Display Pairs of Crystals

Question to Ponder: How can I invite the energy of partnership into my love life?

Answer: Crystals are potent tools in feng shui for amplifying energy. Displaying pairs of crystals, such as rose quartz or amethyst, in your bedroom or Southwest corner invites harmony and strengthens the bond between partners. Pairs symbolise unity and balance in love.

Action: Select two matching crystals that resonate with your intentions for love and relationship energy. Place them together in the Southwest corner of your home or bedside table to promote love and emotional healing. Cleanse the crystals regularly to keep their energy pure and potent.

Tip 30: Hang a Crystal in the Southwest Corner

Question to Ponder: How can I amplify and direct love energy in my home?

Answer: Hanging a crystal, such as clear quartz or rose quartz, in the Southwest corner of your home can amplify the love energy and help direct it where it's most needed. Crystals are natural energy enhancers in feng shui, helping to clear negative energy and promote positivity in relationships.

Action: Hang a faceted crystal in the Southwest corner of your home, preferably near a window that can catch sunlight. This will reflect light and love energy throughout your space, promoting harmony and attraction in your relationship. Clean the crystal regularly to maintain its energy-clearing properties.

Tip 31: Create a Relationship Vision Board

Question to Ponder: How clear am I about my love life goals and intentions?

Answer: A vision board is a powerful tool for manifesting your desires. Creating a feng shui vision board specifically for your love life can clarify your relationship goals and attract the kind of partnership you desire. It helps you stay focused on your love and relationship aspirations.

Action: Gather images, words, and symbols representing the relationship you want to cultivate. Place these on a board, focusing on what you wish to manifest in your love life. Display this board in your bedroom or the Southwest corner to strengthen your intentions and attract the desired energy into your life.

Tip 32: Avoid Work-Related Items in the Bedroom

Question to Ponder: Does my bedroom genuinely serve as a sanctuary for love and rest, or is it filled with distractions?

Answer: Work-related items like laptops, files, and paperwork introduce the energy of stress and productivity into your bedroom, disrupting its primary purpose of love, rest, and rejuvenation. These items can block romantic energy and strain the emotional bond between partners.

Tip 25: Use Dragon and Phoenix for Harmonious Union

Question to Ponder: How can I cultivate a harmonious, balanced relationship with my partner?

Answer: In feng shui, the Dragon and Phoenix symbolise marital bliss and harmony. Together, they represent the perfect balance of masculine (yang) and feminine (yin) energies, creating a harmonious union between partners.

Action: Place a pair of Dragon and Phoenix figurines in the Southwest corner of your home or bedroom to enhance your relationship's balance and harmony. If you're single, these symbols can also help attract a well-matched partner who complements your energy. Make sure both figures are displayed together, as separation can disrupt the balance.

Tip 26: Avoid Bed Facing the Door

Question to Ponder: Does the positioning of my bed invite restful sleep and intimacy?

Answer: In feng shui, a bed directly facing the door is known as the "coffin position," which is considered inauspicious as it invites unsettling energy. This can lead to disturbed sleep and imbalance in your relationship. It also creates a sense of vulnerability, exposing your energy to the outside world.

Action: If your bed is directly aligned with the door, consider repositioning it. If moving the bed is impossible, use a solid headboard or a room divider to block the direct energy flow from the door to the bed. This will create a more secure, intimate space for rest and connection.

Tip 27: Choose Bed Linens with Care

Question to Ponder: How do the textures and colours in my bedroom affect my relationship energy?

Answer: The fabrics and colours of your bed linens can influence the energy in your relationship. Soft, luxurious textures invite comfort and intimacy, while harsh or cold materials may create distance. The colours of your linens also play a role in setting the emotional tone in your bedroom.

Action: Choose soft, high-quality linens in warm, inviting colours like pink, peach, or red. These colours enhance romantic energy and strengthen the emotional connection between partners. Avoid stark white or overly dark tones, which may dampen the warm energy needed for love and intimacy.

Tip 28: Honor the Presence of Two

Question to Ponder: Does my home reflect my desire for a balanced and equal partnership?

Answer: In feng shui, the number two is strongly associated with partnerships and balance. Creating an environment that reflects the presence of two allows for equality and harmony in your love life. Objects that come in pairs promote unity and shared energy between partners.

Action: Ensure that essential areas of your home, especially the bedroom, reflect this concept of two. Place two nightstands, two pillows, and pairs of decor items like candles, lamps, or artwork. This symmetry fosters balance and equality in your relationship, helping both partners feel valued and supported.

Tip 29: Avoid Storage Under the Bed

Question to Ponder: Am I unknowingly blocking the flow of love energy in my relationship?

Answer: Storage under the bed can block energy flow, creating stagnation in your love life. It can lead to feeling stuck, emotionally overwhelmed, or disconnected from your partner. This is especially true if the items stored under the bed relate to work or past relationships.

Action: Clear out any items stored under your bed, especially those related to work, finances, or old memories. Keeping this area clean and open allows energy to flow freely and fosters a restful, loving environment. If storage is unavoidable, ensure it is limited to soft, neutral items like extra linens or pillows.

Action: Remove all work-related items from your bedroom. If you must work in this space, try to separate it with a screen or use designated storage to hide these items when not in use. Prioritise creating a peaceful, loving environment that supports intimacy and relaxation.

Tip 33: Use Sound Therapy for Love

Question to Ponder: How can I clear emotional blocks and invite harmony into my relationship?

Answer: Sound therapy is a powerful Feng Shui tool for clearing stagnant energy and balancing emotional vibrations. Certain sounds, like bells, chimes, or singing bowls, can help release emotional blocks, promote harmony, and invite loving energy into your home.

Action: Use a Tibetan singing bowl or chimes in the Southwest corner of your home or bedroom to clear the space and invite new, vibrant love energy. Ring bells or play soft music to maintain a high frequency of love and peace in your home. Regular sound therapy sessions can help deepen emotional connections with your partner.

Tip 34: Activate Relationship Luck with Double Happiness Symbol

Question to Ponder: How can I strengthen the bond of joy and happiness in my love life?

Answer: The Double Happiness symbol in Feng Shui is a traditional Chinese character representing joy and happiness, particularly in relationships and marriage. It amplifies love energy and helps to create a harmonious, joyful union.

Action: Display the Double Happiness symbol in the Southwest corner of your home or bedroom, or wear it as jewellery to attract love and happiness. This symbol is potent for those seeking to deepen their romantic relationships or enhance the joy within an existing partnership.

Tip 35: Use Red Candles for Passion

Question to Ponder: How can I reignite passion and romantic energy in my relationship?

Answer: Red is the colour of passion, love, and vitality. In Feng Shui, lighting red candles can activate romantic and passionate energy in your space. Candles also carry the Fire element, which helps reignite intimacy and connection between partners.

Action: Light red candles in your bedroom or the Southwest corner during moments of romance or when you want to spark passion. Be mindful of the candle's placement—ensure they are in pairs to represent balanced love. Let the candle's warmth and glow enhance your relationship's passion.

Tip 36: Incorporate Soft Textures for Intimacy

Question to Ponder: How can I create a bedroom that invites closeness and tenderness?

Answer: The textures in your bedroom are important in inviting closeness and tenderness. Soft, inviting materials like plush fabrics, silk, or velvet help create a nurturing, sensual environment that supports emotional connection and intimacy.

Action: Introduce soft, luxurious textures into your bedroom decor. Use silky sheets, velvet throw pillows, or a plush rug to make your space feel cozy and inviting. Soft textures soothe the senses and encourage feelings of comfort and connection, making it easier to relax and bond with your partner.

Tip 37: Promote Relationship Growth with Bamboo

Question to Ponder: How can I foster steady growth and resilience in my love life?

Answer: Bamboo is a powerful symbol of growth, flexibility, and resilience in Feng Shui. Its solid yet flexible nature represents a relationship that can grow and withstand challenges. Bamboo in your home encourages steady, healthy growth in your love life.

Action: Place a lucky bamboo plant in the Southwest corner of your home to promote continuous growth in your relationship. Bamboo also enhances patience and flexibility between partners, helping both of you bend but not break when facing obstacles. Make sure the plant is healthy and thriving, as this reflects the strength of your relationship.

Tip 38: Position Your Bed Against a Solid Wall

Question to Ponder: Does my relationship feel supported and protected, or is it vulnerable to outside forces?

Answer: In Feng Shui, positioning your bed against a solid wall represents the support and protection your relationship needs to thrive. A bed without a solid backing or one placed under a window can create feelings of vulnerability or insecurity in love.

Action: Ensure your bed is positioned against a solid wall rather than under a window or open space. This provides energetic support and a feeling of safety in your relationship. If you cannot move the bed, use a solid headboard to compensate and create a sense of groundedness and protection.

Tip 39: Use Citrine to Attract Love and Happiness

Question to Ponder: How can I bring more joy and positivity into my relationship?

Answer: Citrine is a Feng Shui crystal known for its vibrant energy and ability to attract happiness, love, and abundance. It clears away negative emotions and infuses your space with joyful, positive vibrations, helping to strengthen and brighten relationships.

Action: Place citrine crystals in the Southwest corner or around your home to invite happiness and love into your relationship. Wear citrine jewellery to carry this joyful energy throughout the day. Cleanse the crystals regularly to keep their energy vibrant and compelling.

Tip 40: Avoid Mirrors Facing the Bed

Question to Ponder: How can I ensure my relationship remains private and intimate?

Answer: Mirrors facing the bed can reflect and amplify energy, creating restlessness and potential third-party interference in your relationship. They disrupt the peaceful, intimate energy of your bedroom and invite distractions.

Action: If you have a mirror facing your bed, cover it with a cloth at night or reposition it. Ideally, avoid placing mirrors where they directly reflect the bed. This will help maintain privacy, promote restful sleep, and protect your relationship from external influences.

Tip 41: Create a Love Corner in Your Home

Question to Ponder: How can I designate a unique space focusing solely on love and romance?

Answer: In Feng Shui, creating a dedicated "love corner" in your home invites love energy to flow into your life. This space should be thoughtfully arranged with symbols and objects that represent love, romance, and togetherness.

Action: Choose a small area in the Southwest corner of your home or bedroom to create your love corner. Decorate it with rose quartz, candles, romantic artwork, or paired objects like doves or hearts. Use this space as a visual reminder of your love goals and intentions, and visit it regularly to set new intentions for your relationship.

Tip 42: Use Lavender for Calm and Connection

Question to Ponder: How can I introduce more peace and calm into my relationship?

Answer: Lavender is a calming, soothing herb that promotes peace and harmony. In Feng Shui, its gentle energy helps reduce stress and tension, making it easier to connect with your partner on a deeper level.

Action: Place fresh or dried lavender in your bedroom or use lavender essential oil in a diffuser to create a calm, serene atmosphere. Lavender helps to clear away stress, allowing you and your partner to relax and enjoy each other's company. It also promotes restful sleep, further strengthening emotional bonds.

Tip 43: Avoid Ceiling Beams Over the Bed

Question to Ponder: Are there invisible pressures weighing down on my relationship?

Answer: In Feng Shui, ceiling beams above the bed are believed to create oppressive energy, symbolically placing pressure on your relationship. This can lead to stress or tension between partners, as the heavy energy disrupts the balance of love and rest.

Action: If possible, avoid sleeping under exposed ceiling beams. If your bed must be placed there, soften the space by hanging fabric or installing a canopy. This will deflect the heavy energy from the beams and restore peace and balance to your relationship.

Tip 44: Encourage Fresh Air for Vitality

Question to Ponder: How can I refresh the energy of love in my home?

Answer: Stale air can stagnate love energy in your home. Fresh air invites new beginnings and revitalises the romantic atmosphere, helping relationships feel lighter, more vibrant, and alive.

Action: Open windows regularly to let fresh air circulate through your home, especially in the bedroom and the Southwest corner. If weather or conditions don't allow, use an air purifier to keep the air clean and fresh. Incorporating peace lilies or snake plants can also improve air quality and energise love vibrations.

Tip 45: Invite Harmony with White Roses

Question to Ponder: How can I bring more peace and purity into my love life?

Answer: White roses symbolise purity, peace, and clarity in love. In Feng Shui, they can clear emotional baggage and create space for harmony and fresh beginnings in your relationship. White roses calm turbulent emotions and help foster understanding between partners.

Action: Place a vase of fresh white roses in your bedroom or the Southwest corner of your home to promote peaceful, loving energy. If fresh roses aren't available, consider using white rose imagery or dried arrangements to symbolise purity in your love life.

Tip 46: Embrace Circular Shapes for Unity

Question to Ponder: How can I strengthen the sense of unity and togetherness in my relationship?

Answer: Circular shapes in Feng Shui symbolise wholeness, unity, and the cyclical nature of life. These shapes encourage togetherness and smooth out rough edges in a relationship, helping partners feel connected and harmonious.

Action: Incorporate circular decor items, such as round mirrors, vases, or rugs, in your bedroom or the Southwest corner to enhance the sense of unity. These shapes encourage balance and completeness, making it easier for love to flow smoothly between you and your partner.

Tip 47: Create a Love Intention with Affirmations

Question to Ponder: How can I use the power of words to manifest my ideal relationship?

Answer: Words carry energy, and affirmations are a powerful way to set intentions and attract your desired love and relationship. Positive affirmations help shift your mindset and create an environment of love, trust, and openness.

Action: Write down or speak daily affirmations about love and your relationship goals. Place them in the Southwest corner or near your love altar. Some examples include, "I am worthy of deep, fulfilling love," or, "My partner and I share a strong, balanced connection." Repeating these affirmations helps program your space with loving intentions.

Tip 48: Place Family Photos in the Living Room

Question to Ponder: How can I strengthen the love and unity within my family?

Answer: Family photos carry the energy of connection and love. In Feng Shui, displaying these photos in the living room—the heart of the home—reinforces family bonds and creates a warm, loving atmosphere that benefits all relationships.

Action: Select cherished family photos that symbolise happiness and togetherness and display them in your living room or common area. Avoid placing family photos in the bedroom; this space is meant for romantic intimacy, not family energy. Refresh the photos occasionally to keep the energy current.

Tip 49: Incorporate Water Features Mindfully

Question to Ponder: How can I use water flow to enhance my love life without overwhelming it?

Answer: Water features in Feng Shui symbolise the flow of wealth and emotions. While water can encourage smooth, calm emotional energy, too much water in the wrong places can overwhelm love and lead to imbalance.

Action: If you wish to include a water feature, place it outside the bedroom, such as in the living room or garden, where its energy will flow more appropriately. Ensure the water flows gently and steadily. Avoid stagnant water, representing stuck emotions, and keep the water feature clean and well-maintained.

Tip 50: Use Dragon Tortoise for Lasting Love

Question to Ponder: How can I ensure that my relationship stands the test of time?

Answer: The Dragon Tortoise is a Feng Shui symbol that combines the dragon's strength with the tortoise's longevity. It represents lasting love and endurance in relationships and encourages stability and long-term commitment.

Action: Place a Dragon Tortoise figurine in the Southwest corner of your home or a location central to your relationship. This will strengthen the energy of endurance, helping you and your partner weather challenges and grow stronger together. If you're single, this symbol can attract a partner who shares your long-term goals.

Tip 51: Infuse Love Energy with Pink

Question to Ponder: How can I use colour to attract gentleness and romance?

Answer: In Feng Shui, pink is the colour of love, softness, and compassion. It encourages tenderness and understanding in relationships, helping to open the heart and bring emotional healing.

Action: Introduce pink into your bedroom decor through bedding, pillows, or artwork. Even small touches of pink, such as fresh flowers or candles, can enhance the energy of love in your space. Pair it with soft lighting to create a warm, nurturing atmosphere that supports emotional intimacy.

Tip 52: Enhance Fertility with Pomegranates

Question to Ponder: How can I enhance my relationship's potential for growth and new beginnings, fostering a sense of hope and optimism?

Answer: In feng shui, pomegranates symbolise fertility, abundance, and new beginnings. They represent a relationship's fruitful potential, making them an excellent choice for couples trying to conceive or grow their relationship in new directions.

Action: Place a pomegranate figurine or artwork featuring pomegranates in the Southwest corner of your home to enhance fertility and new opportunities in your love life. This symbol encourages the growth of a family and new dimensions of love and happiness in your relationship.

Tip 53: Avoid Clutter in the Southwest Corner

Question to Ponder: Is there clutter blocking love energy in my home?

Answer: Clutter in the Southwest corner, which governs love and relationships in feng shui, blocks the flow of romantic energy. This can lead to confusion, stagnation, or difficulty attracting or maintaining love.

Action: Commit to clearing all clutter from the Southwest corner of your home. This includes unnecessary items, piles of paperwork, or anything that doesn't contribute to your love goals. By keeping this space clean, organised, and dedicated to love-enhancing objects like crystals, candles, or romantic symbols, you demonstrate your determination to unblock love energy and attract or maintain love.

Tip 54: Attract Love with Peony Flowers

Question to Ponder: How can I invite admiration and romantic attention into my life?

Answer: Peony flowers are one of the most potent feng shui symbols for attracting love and admiration. Their lush, full blooms represent beauty and romance, making them particularly useful for singles seeking new romantic opportunities. By displaying peonies, you can increase your attractiveness and draw new love into your life, empowering you to take control of your romantic destiny.

Action: Display fresh or artificial peonies in your home, particularly in the Southwest corner of your bedroom. If fresh flowers aren't available, artwork featuring peonies will also work. This will invite admiration and increase your attractiveness, helping to draw new love into your life.

Tip 55: Strengthen Communication with Amethyst

Question to Ponder: How can I improve communication and understanding in my relationship?

Answer: Amethyst, a crystal known for its association with clarity and spiritual communication, is a powerful tool in feng shui. It aids in strengthening emotional understanding and fostering open, honest conversations between partners, thereby improving the quality of your relationship.

Action: Place an amethyst crystal in the Southwest corner of your bedroom to enhance the energy of clear communication and emotional clarity. You can also wear amethyst jewellery during essential discussions with your partner to promote understanding and resolve misunderstandings.

Tip 56: Balance Relationship Energy with Yin and Yang Symbols

Question to Ponder: How can I balance giving and receiving more in my relationship?

Answer: The Yin-Yang symbol, representing the balance of opposites in feng shui, is crucial in maintaining balance in relationships. It reminds us that relationships require a delicate balance between the masculine (yang) and feminine (yin) energies, ensuring both partners give and receive equally.

Action: Display a Yin-Yang symbol in your home to remind yourself and your partner of the importance of balance in your relationship. This will empower both of you to focus on open communication and equality, ensuring both partners feel supported and empowered.

Tip 57: Invite Compassion with Lotus Flowers

Question to Ponder: How can I introduce more compassion and understanding into my relationship?

Answer: The lotus flower, a symbol of purity, growth, and compassion in feng shui, is a powerful promoter of emotional healing and understanding. It encourages spiritual development and fosters an environment of unconditional love and learning in your relationship.

Action: Place a lotus flower or artwork featuring lotus flowers in the Southwest corner of your bedroom to cultivate compassion and spiritual connection with your partner. This symbol promotes emotional healing and deepens the bond between partners through kindness and empathy.

Tip 58: Enhance Emotional Security with a Solid Headboard

Question to Ponder: Does my relationship feel supported and secure, or are there gaps in our connection?

Answer: A solid headboard symbolises strength, stability, and support in a relationship. In feng shui, it acts as a metaphor for a relationship's foundation. A weak or absent headboard may indicate instability or lack of support in your love life.

Action: If you do not have a solid headboard, consider investing in one. It should be made from a single piece of wood or upholstered fabric, avoiding headboards with gaps or bars. This will energetically strengthen your relationship's foundation, providing emotional security for both partners.

Tip 59: Use Coral for Emotional Resilience

Question to Ponder: How can I ensure my relationship remains resilient and adaptable?

Answer: Coral symbolises emotional resilience and protection in feng shui. It supports relationships through challenging times and helps partners remain flexible and strong.

Action: Place coral (natural or as a decorative object) in the Southwest corner or bedroom to boost emotional resilience in your relationship. This symbol benefits couples going through stressful periods, as it offers protection and strengthens emotional bonds, fostering resilience in the face of challenges.

Tip 60: Invite Trust with Lapis Lazuli

Question to Ponder: How can I build more profound trust in my relationship?

Answer: Lapis lazuli is a crystal of truth and trust, known in feng shui for enhancing communication and honesty in relationships. It fosters deeper trust between partners by encouraging open, truthful conversations.

Action: Place lapis lazuli crystals in the Southwest corner of your home or bedroom to build trust and honesty in your relationship. You can also meditate with this crystal to gain insight into areas where trust needs strengthening. This energy will help you and your partner feel more connected and aligned, strengthening your bond.

Tip 61: Avoid Heavy Objects Overhead

Question to Ponder: Are there invisible pressures in my relationship that need to be released?

Answer: Heavy objects hung over your bed, such as large artwork or light fixtures, create energetic pressure in feng shui. This pressure can manifest in your relationship as unresolved conflicts or emotional burdens.

Action: Remove heavy objects above your bed to release energetic pressure. Instead, hang light, uplifting artwork that promotes love and harmony. Clearing the space above your bed allows for emotional freedom and helps ease relationship tension.

Tip 62: Strengthen Love with the Fire Element

Question to Ponder: How can I rekindle the warmth and passion in my relationship?

Answer: The Fire element in feng shui symbolises passion, warmth, and energy. If your relationship feels relaxed or disconnected, introducing the Fire element can help reignite intimacy and emotional warmth.

Action: Add fire-element decor, such as red candles, artwork with fiery colours, or a fireplace, to your bedroom or the Southwest corner. Be mindful of balance—too much Fire can lead to conflict, so use this element strategically to spark passion without overwhelming the relationship.

Tip 63: Promote Balance with Paired Crystals

Question to Ponder: How can I ensure equal partnership and mutual respect in my relationship?

Answer: Paired crystals symbolise balance and equality in feng shui. They represent a harmonious energy exchange between partners and encourage mutual respect and support.

Action: Place two identical crystals, such as rose quartz or amethyst, on either side of your bed or in the Southwest corner to symbolise equality. This will encourage balanced energy in your relationship, allowing both partners to feel seen, valued, and supported.

Tip 64: Clear Negative Energy with Sage Smudging

Question to Ponder: Is there any lingering negative energy that needs to be cleared from my relationship space?

Answer: Sage smudging is a powerful feng shui tool for clearing negative energy and creating space for fresh, positive vibrations. Regularly clearing stagnant or negative energy from your home allows love and connection to flow freely.

Action: Use a sage stick to smudge the bedroom and Southwest corner of your home. As you move through these spaces, set an intention for clearing any old, stagnant energy and inviting new love and positive emotions. Repeat this ritual regularly, especially after arguments or stressful periods, to keep the energy fresh and vibrant.

Tip 65: Create a Clear Pathway to Your Front Door

Question to Ponder: Is the entrance to my home inviting and open, allowing love to flow freely into my life?

Answer: A clear, welcoming entrance invites positive chi and new love energy into your home. Cluttered or blocked pathways can symbolically block opportunities for love.

Action: Ensure the pathway to your front door is clutter-free, well-lit, and inviting. Place plants or soft lighting on either side of the entrance to guide love energy into your home.

Tip 66: Incorporate the Double Happiness Symbol

Question to Ponder: How can I invite more joy and union into my love life?

Answer: The Double Happiness symbol is not just a symbol; it's a beacon of hope for marital bliss and harmony. It can enhance the energy of love and joy in relationships, bringing a sense of optimism and happiness to your love life.

Action: Display the Double Happiness symbol in your Southwest corner or bedroom to amplify marital happiness and emotional connection.

Tip 67: Avoid Clutter Under Your Bed

Question to Ponder: Is there emotional or physical baggage hiding in my relationship?

Answer: Storing items under your bed can create stagnant energy, leading to unresolved relationship issues. By clearing this space, you take control of the energy flow in your relationship, allowing love and connection to flow easily.

Action: Clear items under your bed to promote restful sleep and free-flowing relationship energy.

Tip 68: Activate Love with a Crystal Heart

Question to Ponder: How can I nurture more tenderness and love in my relationships?

Answer: A heart-shaped crystal symbolises love and emotional healing. It magnifies romantic energy and deepens emotional bonds.

Action: Place a rose quartz or amethyst heart in the Southwest corner of your home or on your bedside table to strengthen emotional connections.

Tip 69: Use Earth Elements for Stability in Love

Question to Ponder: How grounded and stable do I feel in my relationships?

Answer: The Earth element brings grounding, stability, and nurturing energy, which is essential for lasting relationships.

Action: Introduce Earth elements like ceramic pots, stone objects, or earthy tones into your bedroom or Southwest corner to promote emotional stability in love.

Tip 70: Incorporate Fresh Flowers for Romantic Vibrancy

Question to Ponder: How can I bring more freshness and vibrancy into my love life?

Answer: Fresh flowers are a decorative element and a source of vitality, beauty, and positive chi. By placing them in the Southwest corner of your living space or bedroom, you can refresh the romantic energy in your relationship, bringing a sense of renewal and excitement to your love life.

Action: Place fresh, vibrant flowers in the Southwest corner of your living space or bedroom to refresh the romantic energy in your relationship. Replace them regularly to keep the energy fresh.

Tip 71: Activate Love Energy with Mandarin Ducks

Question to Ponder: How can I bring more loyalty and harmony into my love life?

Answer: Mandarin ducks are a traditional feng shui symbol of love, loyalty, and lifelong partnership.

Action: Place a pair of mandarin duck figurines in your bedroom or Southwest corner to attract or strengthen lasting romantic partnerships.

Tip 72: Balance Yin and Yang in Your Home

Question to Ponder: Is there a healthy balance of masculine and feminine energy in my relationship?

Answer: A balanced flow of yin (feminine) and yang (masculine) energies ensures harmony in your relationship.

Action: Ensure your home decor includes soft, flowing elements (yin) like curtains, rugs, and round-shaped furniture, and solid and structured elements (yang) like square-shaped furniture, tall plants, and artwork with solid lines to create balance in love.

Tip 73: Enhance Bedroom Lighting for Intimacy

Question to Ponder: How does the lighting in my bedroom affect the emotional warmth in my relationship?

Answer: Soft, warm lighting in the bedroom promotes intimacy and emotional warmth, creating a relaxing and loving environment.

Action: Replace harsh, bright lighting with soft, warm lamps or candles to create a cozy and intimate atmosphere in your bedroom.

Tip 74: Use Mirrors Mindfully in the Bedroom

Question to Ponder: Are mirrors in my bedroom creating tension or imbalance in my relationship?

Answer: Mirrors can disrupt the flow of energy in the bedroom, leading to restlessness or disharmony in relationships.

Action: Avoid placing mirrors that reflect the bed. Mirrors that reflect the bed are believed to disrupt energy flow, leading to restlessness or disharmony in relationships. If you have mirrors in your bedroom, cover them at night to prevent energy disturbances.

Tip 75: Position Your Bed for Relationship Harmony

Question to Ponder: Is the placement of my bed supporting or hindering love and relationship energy?

Answer: The placement of your bed directly impacts the harmony and flow of energy in your relationship.

Action: Ensure your bed is placed in the command position. This means it should be diagonally across from the door but not directly in line with it. This position allows you to see the door while in bed, which is believed to enable positive relationship energy to flow.

Tip 76: Enhance Romance with Soft Bedding

Question to Ponder: Is my bedroom a sanctuary for romance and comfort?

Answer: Soft, luxurious bedding enhances the feeling of intimacy and provides a comforting sanctuary, creating a loving and inviting atmosphere.

Action: Choose soft, high-quality fabrics in romantic colours like pink, peach, or white to encourage relaxation and emotional closeness in your bedroom.

Tip 77: Use Red to Ignite Passion

Question to Ponder: How can I reignite passion and excitement in my relationship?

Answer: In feng shui, red is not just a colour; it's a catalyst for passion, excitement, and love, igniting the fire element in your love life.

Action: Add red accents to your bedroom, such as candles, pillows, or artwork, to reignite passion and emotional warmth in your relationship.

Tip 78: Activate the Love Corner with Paired Crystals

Question to Ponder: How can I create balance and harmony in my love life?

Answer: Crystals in pairs symbolise balance, unity, and equality in love, fostering mutual respect and understanding in relationships.

Action: Place two identical crystals, such as rose or clear quartz, in the Southwest corner of your home. In feng shui, the Southwest corner is associated with love and relationships, making it an ideal spot to create balance in your relationship energy.

Tip 79: Create a Love Intention with Red Roses

Question to Ponder: How can I attract more love and passion into my life?

Answer: Red roses are a classic symbol of love and passion, helping to enhance romantic energy and deepen emotional connections.

Action: Place fresh or artificial red roses in the Southwest corner of your bedroom or living space to invite passion and romance into your life.

Tip 80: Use Metal Elements for Clarity in Communication

Question to Ponder: How clear and open is the communication in my relationship?

Answer: The Metal element is not just about decor; it's about fostering clear communication, focus, and understanding, essential for a harmonious relationship.

Action: Incorporate Metal elements, such as round objects, metallic decor, or white and grey colours, into your Southwest corner to promote honest communication in love.

Tip 81: Activate the Relationship Sector with Earth Colors

Question to Ponder: How can I create more emotional stability and grounding in my relationship?

Answer: Earth tones create a nurturing, stable environment, promoting emotional security and grounded connections in relationships.

Action: Use earthy colours such as beige, brown, and soft yellow in your bedroom or Southwest corner to create a foundation of stability in your love life.

Tip 82: Clear Stagnant Energy with Incense or Sage

Question to Ponder: Is any negative or stagnant energy in my home blocking love from flourishing?

Answer: Stagnant energy, caused by clutter, negative emotions, or lack of fresh air, can block the flow of love and harmony in your relationships. Clearing this energy allows for fresh, positive love energy to flow.

Action: Use sage, incense, or sound cleansing in your home, particularly in the Southwest corner, to clear any stagnant energy and create space for new love.

Tip 83: Create Space for Love in Your Closet

Question to Ponder: Is there room in my life and home to welcome new love or deepen existing connections?

Answer: A cluttered closet can symbolise a lack of space for love and intimacy.

Action: Clear out your closet, leaving space for new love to enter your life. Remove old, unused items and create room for new opportunities and relationships.

Tip 84: Strengthen Love Luck with Feng Shui Symbols

Question to Ponder: How can I use powerful feng shui symbols to attract more love and romance?

Answer: Feng shui symbols like the Double Happiness symbol, which represents double joy and harmony in relationships; Mandarin ducks, which symbolise love and fidelity; and rose quartz, a stone of love, amplifies love energy and creates harmony in relationships.

Action: Place feng shui love symbols in critical areas of your home, such as the Southwest corner or bedroom, to activate and enhance love luck.

Tip 85: Use the Fire Element to Warm Relationships

Question to Ponder: How can I bring more warmth and excitement into my relationship?

Answer: The Fire element is associated with passion, excitement, and emotional warmth, which can ignite and sustain romantic energy.

Action: Introduce elements of fire, such as candles, red accents, or fiery artwork, into your bedroom to rekindle passion and strengthen emotional warmth.

Tip 86: Place Your Bed Away from Windows

Question to Ponder: Does the placement of my bed support restful sleep and emotional security in my relationship?

Answer: Beds placed under or next to windows can create feelings of instability or emotional vulnerability in relationships.

Action: Move your bed away from windows or use heavy curtains to block energy from escaping through the windows, creating

---

Tip 87: Boost Relationship Energy with Paired Candles

Question to Ponder: How can I foster more equality and harmony in my relationship?

Answer: Paired candles, a powerful symbol of balance and equal energy exchange in relationships, can be a catalyst for enhancing unity and partnership.

Action: Place two candles in the Southwest corner of your home or on your bedside table. Light them together to symbolise mutual respect, equality, and shared love.

Tip 88: Introduce Water Elements for Emotional Flow

Question to Ponder: How can I encourage better emotional flow and communication in my relationship?

Answer: Water elements, the essence of emotional flow, can be a key to releasing emotional blockages and fostering better communication in relationships.

Action: Place a small fountain or water feature in your living space (not the bedroom) to encourage emotional openness and improve communication with your partner.

Tip 89: Add Wooden Furniture for Growth

Question to Ponder: How can I nurture growth and stability in my romantic relationships?

Answer: Wood symbolises growth, vitality, and expansion. Incorporating it can help relationships flourish and strengthen.

Action: Add wooden furniture or decor to your Southwest corner or living space. This will encourage emotional growth and foster a sense of security and stability in your relationship.

Tip 90: Strengthen Relationships with Fresh Air and Light

Question to Ponder: Is the energy in my home stagnant, blocking the flow of love and connection?

Answer: Fresh air and natural light create vitality and allow love energy to circulate freely, nurturing your relationships.

Action: Open your windows regularly to invite fresh air into your space. Use sheer curtains to maximise natural light and keep the energy flowing smoothly in your home.

Tip 91: Remove Sharp Objects to Soften Love Energy

Question to Ponder: Are there sharp objects in my home that may create tension in my relationship?

Answer: Sharp objects or furniture edges create harsh energy that can lead to tension or arguments in relationships.

Action: Remove or soften sharp objects in your bedroom and living space. Use rounded furniture, cushions, or fabric to create a more nurturing and loving atmosphere.

Tip 92: Use the Phoenix Symbol to Reignite Passion

Question to Ponder: How can I reignite passion and renewal in my relationship?

Answer: The phoenix, a potent symbol of rebirth and transformation, can be a powerful tool for helping relationships overcome challenges and emerge stronger.

Action: Place a phoenix symbol in your bedroom or Southwest corner to invite renewal, passion, and transformation in your romantic life.

Tip 93: Balance Your Bedroom with Natural Elements

Question to Ponder: Does my bedroom create a harmonious balance between comfort and romance?

Answer: A balanced bedroom with natural elements like wood, plants, and soft fabrics creates a nurturing space for love and connection.

Action: Add plants, wooden furniture, and soft fabrics to your bedroom to balance the energy and promote harmony and comfort in your relationship.

Tip 94: Activate Love with Romantic Artwork

Question to Ponder: Does the art in my home inspire love, connection, and romance?

Answer: Romantic artwork, such as paintings of couples or peaceful, loving scenes, helps to activate love energy and inspires emotional connection.

Action: Display romantic artwork in your bedroom or Southwest corner to enhance the energy of love and intimacy in your relationship.

Tip 95: Keep the Path to Your Bedroom Clear

Question to Ponder: Is anything physically or emotionally blocking love from flowing into my life?

Answer: A clear, unobstructed path to the bedroom invites positive love energy to flow freely, unimpeded by distractions or obstacles.

Action: Clear the hallway or entryway to your bedroom of clutter. Clearing a path allows love energy to enter your relationship space quickly, creating an open and receptive atmosphere for intimacy and connection.

Tip 96: Use a Pair of Lamps for Balanced Energy

Question to Ponder: Do both partners in my relationship feel equally supported and valued?

Answer: Paired lamps on either side of the bed represent balance and equality in love, fostering mutual respect and emotional support.

Action: Place two matching lamps on either side of your bed to create balanced energy and ensure you and your partner feel equally valued and supported.

Tip 97: Create Space for New Love

Question to Ponder: Is there room in my life and home to invite new love or deepen an existing relationship?

Answer: Leaving physical and emotional space allows love energy to enter your life more freely, inviting new opportunities for connection.

Action: Clear out any old belongings or items that no longer serve you in your bedroom or living space. This creates room for new love to enter or an existing relationship to grow.

Tip 98: Enhance the Bedroom with the Fire Element for Passion

Question to Ponder: How can I add more passion and excitement to my love life?

Answer: The Fire element ignites passion, desire, and emotional warmth, making it an essential energy for romantic relationships.

Action: Add fiery elements, such as red candles, romantic lighting, or warm-coloured bedding, to your bedroom to enhance the energy of passion and intimacy in your love life.

Tip 99: Position Bedside Tables Symmetrically

Question to Ponder: Does my bedroom design promote balance and harmony in my relationship?

Answer: Symmetry in bedroom furniture fosters balance and equality in relationships, helping partners feel equally valued and supported.

Action: Ensure your bedside tables are symmetrically placed and balanced on either side of the bed. This promotes harmony, balance, and mutual respect between partners.

Tip 100: Use Soft Music to Harmonise Love Energy

Question to Ponder: How can I create a calming, loving atmosphere in my home?

Answer: Soft, soothing music helps to harmonise the energy in your home, promoting relaxation, emotional connection, and love.

Action: Play calming, romantic music in your bedroom or living space to create a peaceful and loving atmosphere, which will help deepen emotional bonds and intimacy.

FENG SHUI LOVE AND RELATIONSHIP LUCK CHECKLIST

A GUIDE TO ALIGNING YOUR HOME'S ENERGY FOR LOVE AND RELATIONSHIP SUCCESS

Use this checklist to ensure your home's energy is aligned with love and relationship success. To track your progress, check off each action as you complete it.

1. **Clear Clutter**
   - Remove unnecessary items from key love areas (bedroom, Southwest corner). This step will help you feel relieved and lighter, knowing you are removing obstacles to love.
   - Ensure pathways to doors, especially the front and bedroom, are clear and unobstructed.
   - Declutter under the bed and ensure open space for energy flow.

2. **Enhance the Southwest Corner**
   - Place a pair of symbols (candles, crystals, or artwork) in the Southwest corner to activate love energy.
   - Use Earth elements like ceramics or stones to ground and strengthen relationship energy.
   - Add romantic colours like pinks, reds, and warm tones to boost love energy.

3. **Bedroom Harmony**
   - Ensure the bed is placed in the command position—diagonally across from the door but not directly in line with it.

- Use paired bedside tables and lamps for balance and equality.
- Remove sharp objects or harsh lighting from the bedroom to create a soft, nurturing atmosphere.
- Add soft bedding and textures that promote comfort and intimacy.

4. **Activate Love Symbols**
   - Place meaningful love symbols like rose quartz, heart-shaped objects, or Mandarin ducks in the bedroom or Southwest corner.
   - Display romantic artwork or images of happy couples to enhance emotional connection.
   - Use candles, flowers, or crystals to energise the love area.

5. **Enhance Lighting**
   - Introduce soft, warm lighting to create a cozy, intimate atmosphere in the bedroom.
   - Avoid harsh overhead lighting and use dim lamps or candles instead.
   - Ensure the Southwest corner is well-lit to activate love energy.

6. **Refresh the Energy**
   - Smudge your space with sage or burn incense to clear any stagnant or negative energy.
   - Open windows regularly to let in fresh air and natural light.
   - Add plants or flowers to bring vitality and freshness to your home's love areas.

7. **Mind Your Mirrors**
   - Ensure that mirrors do not reflect the bed, as this can disrupt relationship harmony.
   - Cover mirrors at night if placed near the bed to create a calm and restful environment.

8. **Set Relationship Intentions**
   - Write down your relationship goals or intentions and place them in a visible area to reinforce your desires. This step is crucial in empowering you to take control of your love life.
   - Write down your relationship goals or intentions and place them in a visible area to reinforce your desires.
   - Create a small love altar with symbols representing the love and connection you wish to attract or nurture.

BEGINNERS FENG SHUI
'EASY TIPS TO ENHANCE EVERYDAY LIVING'

A beginner's guide to learning the fundamentals of Feng Shui and energy flow in the home, known as Chi. This ancient art of placement which brings balance, helps to improve the harmony and prosperity within your space. Ideal as a gift for the novice wanting to learn more or beautiful coffee table book to inspire you on your next home renovation.

Buy Beginners Feng Shui   www.completefengshui.com

Ebook Beginners Feng Shui   www.completefengshui.com

BEGINNERS FENG SHUI LOVE AND RELATIONSHIPS
THE BEGINNERS GUIDE TO ATTRACTING LOVE AND ENHANCING RELATIONSHIPS

Beginners Feng Shui Love and Relationships is the ultimate guide and bible for transforming your love life through Feng Shui. This comprehensive 3-part book covers everything from self-realization exercises to enhance your personal growth, every Feng Shui tip imaginable for creating love-filled spaces, and a deep dive into Chinese astrology compatibility. Whether you're attracting new love or nurturing an existing relationship, this book is all you need. Paired with the Feng Shui Love Journal and 100 Feng Shui Love Tips, it's the perfect companion set for mastering love and relationships through Feng Shui.

Buy Beginners Feng Shui Love and Relationships https://bit.ly/4eD9fQe

PERIOD 9 IN FENG SHUI AND CHINESE ASTROLOGY

Explore the potential of Period 9 in Feng Shui and Chinese Astrology from 2024 to 2044. Discover the captivating influence of this twenty-year cycle starting on February 4, 2024. Unleash the power of the Fire Element during Period 9, igniting personal growth, creativity, and innovation. This period offers limitless opportunities and transformation. Learn tailored Feng Shui techniques to align with Period 9's energies, manifesting dreams into reality. Dive into the journey, transforming living or workspaces into vibrant sanctuaries. Stay in sync with cosmic forces using flying stars and dynamic period energy. Join a community of seekers on this life-changing path of growth and prosperity guided by Chinese metaphysics. Embrace Period 9's electrifying power for a transformative journey into a future full of possibilities, altering the trajectory of your life.

Period 9 in Feng Shui and Chinese Astrology www.completefengshui.com

THE FENG SHUI LOVE JOURNAL
A GUIDED WORKBOOK TO ATTRACT LOVE AND ROMANCE INTO YOUR LIFE

Have you enjoyed *100 Feng Shui Love Tips?*

Unlock the transformative power of the *Love and Relationship Self-Help Journal*. More than just a tool, this journal is your dedicated companion on the path to attracting new love, nurturing existing relationships, or deepening self-love. Designed to support personal growth and emotional healing, this journal is essential for anyone seeking meaningful relationship transformations.

Rooted in self-reflection and Feng Shui principles, it offers 365 insightful prompts, questions, and actionable exercises that help you cultivate a life filled with love. From releasing emotional blockages to aligning your home's energy, this journal provides a step-by-step guide to creating harmonious relationships.

Why You Need This Journal:

- Deepen self-awareness and uncover your love patterns
- Heal past wounds and invite fresh, loving energy
- Align your home with Feng Shui to attract love
- Gain clarity on your relationship goals and how to achieve them

Embark on a powerful journey toward emotional fulfillment and lasting love. Let the *Love and Relationship Self-Help Journal* guide you to the deeper connections and harmonious relationships you deserve.
https://bit.ly/3BGfXXO

TESTIMONALS

I have been following Michelle's Feng Shui advice for over 12 years She is an amazing, very professional person with many of her predications being very accurate. **Dot O'Sullivan**

"Michele has a wealth of knowledge of all aspects of feng shui, which she shares with generosity and clarity. She interprets the Chinese astrology charts of each member of the household with great insight and intuitive understanding. Michele is always empathetic to the needs and circumstances of her clients and has helped me and my family tremendously over the many years we have made use of her services. I highly recommend Michele and her work!" **Annie Vorster**

Michele is a True Master of Feng Shui. I have had her involved with my own homes and my workplace's for about 16 or 17 years now.

She is a pleasure to work with and knows so much about Feng Shui, and how to remedy all situations.

Having Feng Shui in my life has helped the energy of my family and workplace, and make them amazing places to want to be, you can feel the calmness and the energy flowing. I am hooked, I love the beginning of every new year, so see what is changed, I love the Bazi Charts you get too, So many interesting things about life and yourself. **Ann Meney**

Great experience with Michele. Very approachable, polite, and friendly. Michele has a lot of Feng Shui knowledge. I feel that I can still ask her questions even after she has completed my consultation and report. Will continue with Michele for all future Feng Shui and interior design matters. **Mary Valentina**

We have been knowing Michele for over 12 years. Always very happy with the Feng Shui readings she does for us yearly, we often refer to and use as guidance throughout each year.

Michele has helped us with the purchase of our homes.

Happily, highly recommended Michele when you need a Feng Shui master for your house, office, and guidance yearly to get you through the year, year after year fan. Michele is very warm, approachable and brings a beautiful energy within her presents. **Aria & Michael Van Uffelen**

Michele Castle is an amazing Fengshui master and has done a very detailed informative book for my home and family. The detailed charts and reports gave us great insight, her amazing experience and explanations help guide us with what the energy is bringing with the year and elements. It has helped us be best prepared, even for the best Feng Shui for our business and money as well.

I am grateful for Michelle's guidance, and I trust her and highly recommend her to my family and friends for her in-depth Feng Shui knowledge. **Bass Tadros**

I have been fortunate enough to have been introduced to Michele and Feng Shui at least 6 years ago. It came about around the trials and tribulations I was having with the building and surroundings I lived and continue to live in. Well, I took on the recommendation to have her check the place out and was pleasantly surprised at her findings and cures and hence allowing peace and harmony to return to my home again. I have completed some courses with Michele and am amazed at how knowledgeable, intuitive, and magical she is... brilliant Feng shui master in my books. I continue to use her for annual assessment of energy flows etc for my home and other aspects of my life.

Love her work and her as a professional being that she is. I highly recommend Michele as a Feng Shui expert and teacher. **Bhavna Mistry**

Since I first met Michele from Complete Feng Shui eight years ago, she has guided me on energetically restoring my house's virtues, found me a landscape artist to design the Garden of Eden of my dreams and sailed me onto the sweet shores of fulfilling romance. She is my go-to Guru and a master of her craft. **Monica Wood**

Michelle is always helpful and willing to advise what works best for everyone in our household. We have engaged her service for over 10 years now on property purchase and annual readings. She is always friendly and so easy to work with. Highly recommend her service. **Frank Walsh**

ABOUT THE AUTHOR

Michele has been in demand as a Feng Shui consultant for over two decades. She has been trained by Master Raymond Lo (from Hong Kong) and Juliana Abraham (from the Feng Shui Centre in Perth, Western Australia) and has studied with Dato Joey Yap and Lillian Too. Michele maintains her studies each year to ensure she continues to provide clients with the best of her skills. Michele has an uncanny ability to read charts and fantastic insight into people. She combines experience and natural intuition with the multi-layered discipline of Feng Shui to deliver positive client outcomes. Michele's approach is practical, realistic and straightforward. She adores the reward of making a difference in the lives of her valued clients.

Having studied architectural drafting and interior design and working with interiors and renovations on her own homes, it was a natural progression to incorporate Feng Shui and metaphysical studies into those projects. Applauded for her style, Michele was often asked if she could share her gift with others.

Passion and dedication, combined with further studies, saw her first Feng Shui business, Energise Life Feng Shui born and evolve into Complete Feng Shui.

Michele conducts onsite Feng Shui consultations for residential and corporate clients. An accredited teacher at recognised training institutes, author and public speaker with numerous radio and television guest appearances. Michele works alongside families with residential homes, developers, architects, interior designers, real estate agents, restaurants, cafes, day spas and retail stores.

For any existing or proposed business client Michele can help with staff recruitment, choosing the best location and orientation for business premises, improving the atmosphere and working environment, and advisement on business stationery such as letterheads and business cards.

For the residential client, Michele offers guidance on improving health and harmony in the home, choosing the best home for you and improving the chances of selling your home. Other services include how to select a suitable carer for children or elderly family members and how to improve children's behaviour, sleep and studies.

Michele's practice and qualifications include Classical, Form, 8 Mansions, 24 Mountain Compass, and Flying Star School Feng Shui. Site selection and design. Metaphysical studies of Four Pillars of Destiny / Bazi / Pa Chee, Qi Men, Millionaires Feng Shui with particular interest and studies on Feng Shui Love and relationship luck.

Michele teaches beginner to practitioner Feng Shui seminars, workshops, courses and retreats and conducts onsite learning experiences at homes and businesses. Students receive complete course notes. There are courses to explore for those who have mastered the basics of Feng Shui and wish to continue their studies and share their knowledge.

With an ability to relate to people from all walks of life. Based in Perth, but regularly consulting in Singapore, Bali and eastern states of Australia on residential, business, and commercial properties.

Michele truly believes:

"Life is what our thoughts, environment and energy make it". "Change your environment and thoughts; change your life".

With knowledge of Feng Shui, it can work to increase wealth, enhance health, and harmonise relationships.

Transform and Empower Your Love Life: A Love Reset Retreat in Bali-A Unique Opportunity to Reset Your Love Life

Ready to attract the relationship you've always dreamed of? Join Feng Shui Love specialist Michele Castle for an extraordinary retreat in Bali to help you transform your love life by aligning your mind, body, and surroundings. Dive into six days of indulgence and self-discovery in a traditional Balinese resort, where you'll learn how to unlock the secrets to lasting love and relationship harmony and discover more about yourself than you ever thought possible.

What Awaits You:
- **6 Days of Bliss:** Shop, relax, enjoy cocktails, and savour delicious cuisine as you soak in the beauty of Bali.
- **Authentic Chinese Bazi Love Profiling:** Discover your unique love potential and fast-track your future possibilities.
- **Enhance Relationship Harmony:** Learn Feng Shui principles to improve love and relationships.
- **Vibrate with Love & Abundance:** Tap into your unique energy to attract love and prosperity.
- **Indulge in a Spa Package:** Enjoy a 2-hour footbath, reflexology, massage, and body scrub.
- **Create Your Signature Scent:** Participate in a French Perfume workshop.
- **Culinary Adventure:** Take part in a traditional Indonesian cooking class.
- **Healing & Meditation:** Experience a healing day ceremony, water purification, meditation, and more.
- **Cultural Exploration:** Discover Ubud's rich culture, vibrant markets, and exquisite dining.
- **Sound Healing at the Pyramids of Chi:** Immerse yourself in a divine sound healing session.
- **Jewellery-Making Workshop:** Unleash your creativity in a fun and unique setting.
- **Luxury Accommodation:** Stay at a boutique-style hotel, with breakfast, teas, and airport transfers included.

Rejuvenate your soul and reconnect with what makes you unique. This retreat allows you to reset your love life and embrace the love you deserve.

Visit https://completelifestyleretreat.com.au/ or https://www.facebook.com/completelifestyleretreats to explore past retreats.

Take this time for yourself. Your love life is waiting to be transformed!

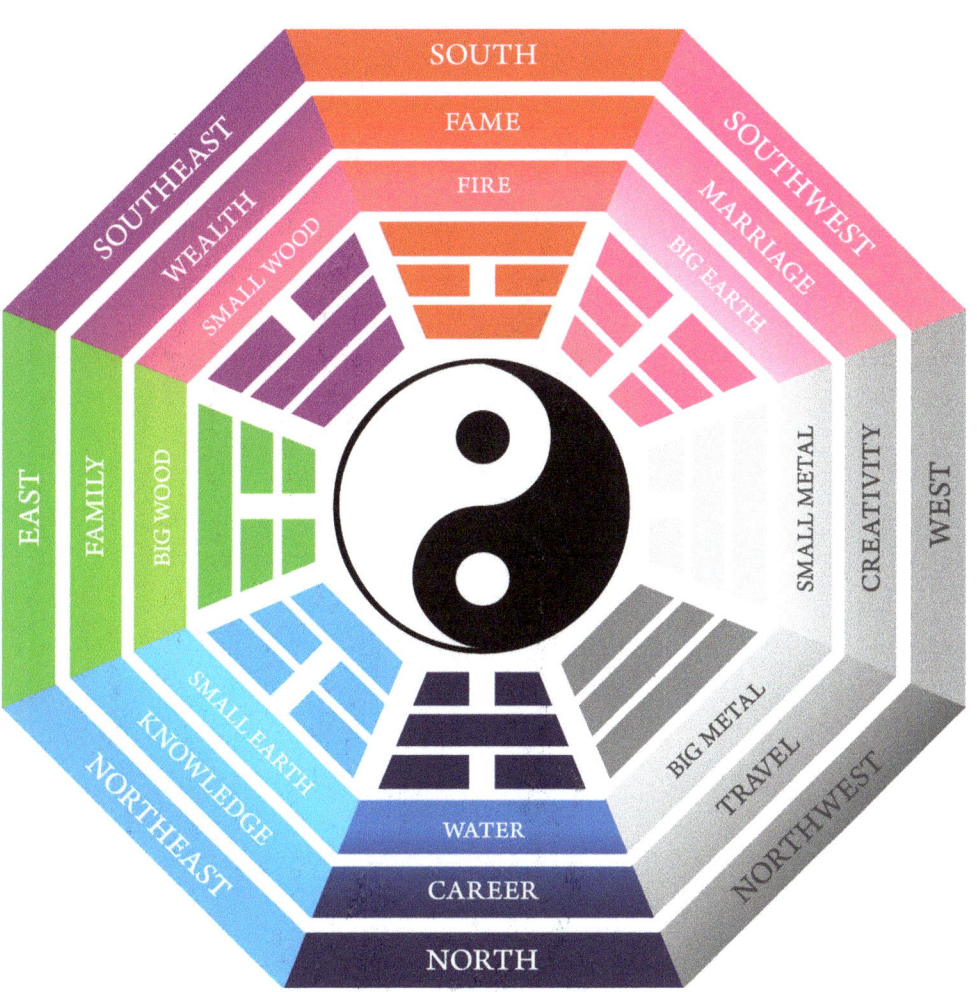

www.ingramcontent.com/pod-product-compliance
Lightning Source LLC
Chambersburg PA
CBHW062041290426
44109CB00026B/2697